HOME PORT COOKBOOK

Lorrie & Jerry

Hope you enjoy
Fair Winds,

Will Holt

HOME PORT COOKBOOK

BELOVED RECIPES FROM MARTHA'S VINEYARD

WILL HOLTHAM

with

A. D. MINNICK

Food photography by Mike Buytas | Illustrations by Susan Tobey White

Forewords by James Taylor, Michael J. Fox, Linda Fairstein,
Judy Belushi Pisano, and Stan Hart

 Lyons Press | Guilford, Connecticut | An imprint of Globe Pequot Press

Lyons Press is an imprint of Globe Pequot Press.

Images on pp. vi, viii, xviii, 3, 4, 12, 15, 18, 22, 34, 104, 135, 213, and 218 courtesy Will Holtham.

Project editor: Gregory Hyman
Text design: Sheryl P. Kober
Layout artist: Melissa Evarts

Library of Congress Cataloging-in-Publication Data

Holtham, Will.
   Home Port Cookbook : Beloved Recipes from Martha's Vineyard / By Will Holtham with A. D. Minnick ; Food Photography by Mike Buytas ; Illustrations by Susan Tobey White.
      pages cm
   Includes index.
   ISBN 978-0-7627-5986-6
   1. Cooking (Sefood) 2. Home Port (Restaurant : Martha's Vineyard, Mass.) 3. Cookbooks.
I. Title.
   TX747.H65 2011
   641.6'92—dc22   2010042983

Printed in China

10 9 8 7 6 5 4 3 2 1

To Chet and Esther Cummens:
Without your kindness, generosity, and support,
none of this would have been possible.

Chet and Esther Cummens, with daughter Brenda,
circa 1984

But then that smoking chowder came in . . . Oh, sweet friends! hearken to me. It was made of small juicy clams, scarcely bigger than hazel nuts, mixed with pounded ship biscuit, and salted pork cut into little flakes; the whole enriched with butter, and plentifully seasoned with pepper and salt pork.

—*Herman Melville,* Moby Dick

TABLE OF CONTENTS

I still find it hard to believe sometimes it has been more than 40 years since my first summer working at the Home Port. Never in my wildest dreams could I have imagined that summer job would lead to a lifetime passion for cooking—a little bit of which I hope to pass on with this book.

The recipes in this book are a testament to the tried-and-true cooking philosophy that made the Home Port famous so long ago and has ensured its place at the forefront of the ever-changing culinary landscape. The recipes I selected for this book are a combination of Home Port favorites and the stories behind them—like quahog chowder, baked-stuffed lobster, and broiled swordfish—along with some of my favorite recipes with some fun twists along the way. It's cooking at its roots, before the nouvelle techniques that have become so popular in the last twenty years or so. You don't need fancy sauces or presentations to make good food. Cooking doesn't have to be a tedious, difficult, scary profession. Preparing dinner should be as enjoyable as eating it. It's as simple as that.

In Appreciation . . .

BY JAMES TAYLOR

Throughout my childhood, my family would escape from the stifling summer heat of North Carolina to the refreshing Atlantic breezes of Martha's Vineyard. The Island was still a relative secret to the rest of the world. It hadn't been discovered yet. It was quaint and quiet. Not yet the summertime playground for the rich and famous like it is today. Even then the Home Port was part of summertime life on Martha's Vineyard. As much as lazing on the beach and exploring the Gay Head cliffs and sailing on Vineyard Sound, a lobster dinner and piece of blueberry pie at the Home Port were part and parcel of the Vineyard summertime experience. It's a summertime tradition: A tradition that has endured for these many years much to the pleasure and delight of so many. A tradition I am happy to say I was a part of in some small way.

Like so many young people who spent their summers on the Island, the Home Port was not only a place where we ate with our families and friends; it was our employer. It's hard to find someone who lived on the Island that didn't work at the Home Port at some point in time. It was a rite of passage for so many young people on the Island, myself included, one of the handful of jobs I ever held outside of playing music. Over the course of my career people have asked what motivated me to go into music. Suffice it to say, the brief time I spent washing dishes at the Home Port was all the motivation I needed. I earned enough money working there to buy my first electric guitar, a second-hand Silvertone I bought right there on the Island, and an amplifier, and had enough left over to have a good time at the Agricultural Fair.

When it comes to traditional Martha's Vineyard fare—quahog chowder, lobster, broiled bluefish and swordfish—the Home Port was always the only game in town. It's wonderful that there is a place that has remained steadfast in carrying on the Island traditions all these years. It hasn't changed. The Home Port today is the same Home Port where I worked nearly forty years ago. It was an essential pillar of Island life then, and it remains one now. The Home Port embodies summertime on Martha's Vineyard. It's where it resides.

BY JUDY BELUSHI PISANO

Guided by a fortunate stroke of serendipity, my late husband John Belushi and I found Martha's Vineyard in June of 1974. Embarking by ferry, the six-mile crossing was both exciting and calming. The flurry of activity at the dock was nicely juxtaposed with the serenity of the drive up-island where John and I delighted at the discovery of an old Menemsha inn with funky one-room seaside cottages—the perfect setting to stage our sojourn.

We threw ourselves wholeheartedly into the role of the "vacationing couple." Long warm days, hot sex, and cold salty water defined our waking hours, which were easily and enjoyably filled. Many recollections are reduced to a sublime feeling, but one that remains crisp is our dinner at the Home Port.

In search of an authentic and delicious New England–style dinner at an affordable price—we were still struggling artists, after all, and John had visions of ordering a super-meaty-jumbo-mo-fo lobster—we were told the Home Port would fit the bill. There was a weathered look to the place that gave it a sense of dignity. Strategically positioned on the harbor, the restaurant was a giant front-row seat to the sunset. The interior did not try to compete with that. The dining room was large and open, the atmosphere easygoing and friendly, the decor rustic yet nautical. Nothing could be finer. But the strongest image in my mind's eye is John's expression as his three-pound lobster was served.

As we ferried away from our newfound haven to our lives in New York City, we vowed to return. John had already selected the beach house he envisioned we would one day own, just off Lucy Vincent Beach. But a lack of funds put the kibosh on the property dream and an abundance of work detained our return. Remembrances of idyllic days—and that lobster!—remained vivid, a constant rekindling of our promise.

After the second season of *Saturday Night Live*, in June of '77, we finally maneuvered our way back on-island, to a rented house just off Middle Road. Much had changed for us in those few years, but the Island was just as we remembered. As soon as we settled in, we made a date with a lobster. At this point in our journey, it was inevitable that we would return to the Home Port, just as thousands of vacationers who return to Martha's Vineyard have done lo these many years. What I did not know at that time was how interconnected I would become with the Home Port over the next thirty-odd years.

The following summer, we were staying in Lambert's Cove, and my parents joined us for a visit. It was my father's birthday, so we planned a dinner in Edgartown. But due to flight delays, by the time they arrived the restaurant had closed their kitchen. This seemed to be the case for every restaurant I tried. For some reason long forgotten I had little food at the house, and my famished parents hadn't eaten since morning. I decided to throw myself on the mercy of the Home Port take-out: "My parents have just arrived. Please, they are hungry. They are old. Anything—bread, uncooked food, someone's forgotten leftovers. . . ." The young woman who answered was very sorry, but, again, the kitchen was closed. As despair began to sink in, a gentleman, apparently on another extension, interjected, saying he'd take the call. It was Will Holtham, the proprietor, whom I did not know at the time. I repeated my sad tale and he said if we could get there in fifteen minutes, he'd make something up.

We could and we did.

With much gratitude and no concern as to what the meals were, we paid and hurried back to the house. Much to our delight, we found four lobster dinners, and thanked the Fates for the kindness of strangers.

In 1979 John and I bought our beach house in Chilmark. Visits became more frequent and bonds grew stronger. Each return, the tradition of going to the Home Port for the big one was a happy day. And in the process, the Home Port became more than a restaurant. As family and guests joined the ritual—a grand meal, stories shared, a stroll along the harbor—these moments became a piece of the stories we revisit, a thread in the interwoven fabric of our lives.

John died in March of 1982. As my life turned upside down, the call of the Vineyard was clear. I chose to bury him on the island he loved so, and thus numerous family and friends descended upon Martha's Vineyard. I put John's family in our house and rented the Flanders House in Chilmark for myself. The sense of loss the Islanders expressed was overwhelming, as was the support and compassion they selflessly extended. A buffet of food filled a large table in the Flanders's kitchen and was replenished daily by Vineyarders; some I knew and others I didn't. I do remember a good supply of Home Port chowder amongst the victuals.

A few months later I returned to the Vineyard on my own for the first time. I arrived late afternoon and picked up a few necessities, figuring I'd "take out" from the Home Port. Comfort food. The weather was cold and wet—memory fails as to whether it was mud or snow—but I rather like the idea of snow. Well, to make a short story snappy, I placed an order for the food, jumped in my car, and backed into a giant snowbank. Or maybe a huge mud swamp? Either way, I was good and stuck.

I called the Home Port to relay the change in my plans. Damn. Looks like cereal and fruit for dinner . . . Or so I thought. But minutes later, who should arrive, but Will Holtham—and my dinner. Now you might think it was because he was so cheap he wanted to be certain he got paid for the meal? Not the case at all. I was a friend in need. Shortly after Will left, a fine, strapping fellow drove up on a tractor, pulled my car out of trouble, and drove off into the sunset. A friend of Will's? Indeed.

Fast forward to 1991. I have remarried a fine man, Victor Pisano, and we are happy residents of Vineyard Haven. Our family includes a new baby boy and my three stepdaughters. This was our oldest girl Jessica's freshman year and she was quick to become fast friends with a group of Island girls. One of her best friends was also named Jessica. Jessica Holtham.

This is when my relationship with the Home Port took another twist, because my Jessica, through her friendship with Will's Jessica, took a job as a waitress at the restaurant. In fact, about seven of the high school friends all worked together over a six-year period, as did our next oldest daughter, Becca. That first summer, Jessica didn't drive, so I spent many a late afternoon going back and forth on the Home Port taxi route.

What I learned is no surprise, but I always find it interesting to glimpse the inner workings of an establishment; and what struck me is that these kids worked hard. The hours were long and nonstop, and the large trays weighted with shellfish were heavy. When you took the time to watch these young women work the room, it was impressive. And although the work was grueling, they had a blast. They made good money, too, which made everything all the sweeter.

Today, when I turn an eye inward, I see the Home Port hanging in the memory halls of my mind, welcoming, soothing, and filled with fun and light. I remember the kindness of strangers and a friend indeed. I see a group of girls naively jump into a summer job only to grow into confident, hard-working young women, many of whom now are active professionals on the Island. And I see the perfection in its name: Home Port. It was a safe haven, a place where something special flourished, a family.

And so, we close this chapter on the Home Port. But let us not fear to look back over our shoulders and recall what was, because in the remembering we expose the underpinnings of the community, the characters of the time, and the virtues we share. Whatever your connection is to the Home Port—or if you never had the pleasure of meeting her—it is a story worth hearing.

In Appreciation . . .

BY MICHAEL J. FOX

Martha's Vineyard is a very special place for my family. My wife, Tracy, has spent nearly every summer of her life there. She was kind enough to introduce me to the unique, quaint charm of the Vineyard on our honeymoon. The minute I set foot on the Island I was smitten. I still am. I haven't missed a single summer since that first fateful visit twenty-one years ago. It was on the Vineyard all four of our children experienced their first cool splash of the ocean. They played on the beaches and explored the cliffs at Gay Head. The serenity and sheer beauty of the Island inspired us to name our eldest daughter Aquinnah.

I have nothing but wonderful memories of the many summers I have spent on the Island. The people and places have become a patchwork of many fond memories with one constant—kicking the summer off with a feast at the Home Port.

There is something comforting about going back to the Home Port each year and finding it just as we remembered. It's like summer really hasn't started until we see all of those fish on the wall, get a good whiff of the wonderful smells coming from the kitchen, and see the blazing sunsets outside.

Only then does it sink in, you're really there, you know it's really summer. It's easy to forget just how much food you get until you're back for the first time that year. It just keeps coming and coming, and all the while the collection of giant sea-bass on the wall are staring down at you with an approving gaze as you devour one of their long lost relatives. And after dinner, when you feel like you won't eat again for days, out comes the pie. Somehow there's always room for a piece of Home Port pie (I'm partial to the pecan).

The very fact that we entrust our first meal on the Vineyard each year to Will and his amazing crew at the Home Port is a true testament to them. Tracy and her mom, a gourmet and a gourmand, are happy as clams in the kitchen, coming up with one delicious creation after another, but there is just something about dinner at the Home Port that can't quite be re-created. So now that Will has finally decided to share his many culinary secrets with the rest of the world, I not only look forward to kicking off the summer with an amazing dinner at the Home Port, but also to having a little piece of it with me all year long.

In Appreciation . . .

BY LINDA FAIRSTEIN

My mouth begins to water at the mere mention of the Home Port.

It's not just the delicious meals that await you on every occasion—which I am delightfully looking to re-create on my own from the pages of this book—that awaken my joyful memories: It's every sensory delight that accompanies an event at my favorite Vineyard restaurant. I like to get there in time to see the blazing scarlet sun set beyond the Aquinnah hills, walk the Menemsha dock to inhale the salty sea air as the tide runs out through the bight, smell the mix of aromas that drift from the busy kitchen as we approach the familiar screen door—freshly baked bread, lobster and fish, whatever the catch of the day, and the sound of laughter—pure happiness—as friends and families gather to savor the best meal on the Island.

Summer on the Vineyard can't officially begin until the Home Port is open. Many ocean resorts have a similar seafood establishment, but I've never been anywhere that captures the unique spirit of the Home Port. That starts with the people who have created and nurtured that oh-so-special atmosphere for so many decades, Will and

Madeline Holtham. In the kitchen, Will worked shoulder to shoulder with his crew, his well-worn apron nightly proof of his personal dedication to culinary excellence, while out front Madeline ran the constant flow of guests—longtime patrons and first-time tourists—like a conductor leading a symphony orchestra. Even the occasional wait near the raw bar on the patio had its rewards.

Unlike most restaurants of its ilk, the Home Port doesn't just cater to tourists, who are wisely directed there by innkeepers' and friends' recommendations. Dinner at the Home Port is a staple for Islanders and summer people of long standing, workmen and celebrities sitting side-by-side, celebrating special occasions or just wanting a fantastic meal.

My husband, Justin Feldman, has been a summer resident of Martha's Vineyard going on fifty years now. I've been coming half that time, and my introduction to the Island wasn't complete without an inaugural Home Port meal that first May weekend so long ago. Since, I have learned, as so many regulars do, to place my order without even glancing at the menu. Justin is always eager to see the staff at the season's start, admiring the hard-working young adults we have watched graduate from busing tables to the waitstaff. Many balance two tough jobs, somehow conserving strength to carry the enormous trays from the steamy kitchen, nimbly making their way through the crowded dining room, always managing to remain as cheerful as they are efficient. After catching up on their winter, Justin speed-orders his classics: quahog chowder, salad with celery seed dressing, a single boiled lobster with a side of french fries, and always for dessert, the best key lime pie in the world, though really ordering is a technicality. They already know what he likes.

I can't think of a birthday or celebratory event that hasn't been organized around a table at the Home Port. Our grandson's first lobster started an annual tradition, reenacted the night our extended family arrives from their home in the Rockies. By midwinter we discuss with our many friends who spend time on the Island whether our first lobster of the season will be baked-stuffed (my preference) or boiled, each and every one anxiously awaiting their return.

I can't help but smile when I think about the Home Port. To me, it's the very best of Vineyard hospitality, serving up the perfect summer meal to satisfy everyone's taste. You'll have to provide your own sunset and the briny ocean scent that whets my appetite every time I head to Menemsha, but this book will welcome you to the Holthams' table and let you feast with them as we have done for many happy years.

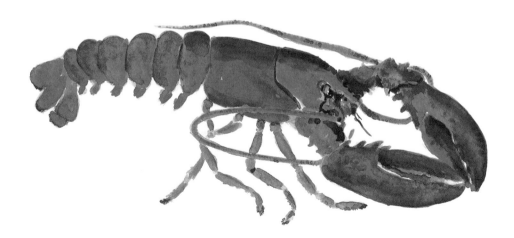

BY STAN HART

In the 1930s, when I was a kid, my parents would take me along for a swim by the foot of the Webosque cliffs on the south shore of Chilmark. It was always a great experience. Roads to Chilmark were unpaved, and going from the top of the cliffs, where my father parked his car, down to the beach took stamina and caution. As a boy, I would find an area where deep sand fronted the ocean side of the cliff and I would roll down to the beach below. Climbing up was tiring for the older folks and a joy to me. To ascend to the top was like climbing to the top of the world.

I mention the cliffs and the beach because inevitably our family swimming parties were followed by a trip to the Home Port for chowder. Martha's Vineyard in the '30s was not as extensive as it is today. The Home Port was an outpost, famous for its chowder and swordfish dinners. As the older folks finished their dinners, I gulped down my chowder so I could go down to the fishing dock for a closer look at the massive swordfish hanging on the halyards that only hours before had been swimming in the vast recesses of the Atlantic, as the proud fishermen posed next to their monstrous catch while tourists snapped photographs, before swaggering to the Home Port and feasting on their catch.

Over the decades, it has been my pleasure to dine at the Home Port in all its configurations, from a glorified clam shack of the '40s and '50s to the expansive edifice it is today. Always I consumed delicious seafood, attended by much merriment, sometimes just two of us but often in larger groups. Through two marriages and several children, I have been a consistent champion of Martha's Vineyard's premier seafood restaurant. Of course the restaurant expanded between my boyhood visits and today, but the food has always remained fresh and tasty, and in its famous sizable helpings. No one ever left the Home Port hungry.

And like so many residents of the charming little island, there was a time I served as a faithful employee at the iconic seafood establishment. For four years I played the role of host at the Home Port. It was great fun to say, "Why of course, Mrs. Pomery, your table for four is ready. Let me lead you to your table, where you will have a meal of succulence the likes of which you will never forget."

It is impossible to forget all of the incredible people I had the pleasure to meet and observe during my time there. Who can forget the actress Daryl Hannah having a hissy fit, leaving John Kennedy Jr. sitting alone to stare into space, or the wonderful, the beautiful Beverly Sills, or Ted Kennedy, a sailor in port, beaming with pleasure, his wife Vicki sitting across from him, the merriment in his heart contagious. Walter Cronkite, Andrew Young, Carly Simon . . . Celebrities mixed with locals and vacationing families—it was truly a joy to observe, and to play some small part in it all.

My friend Will Holtham is retired now, but the restaurant endures. New owners will try to equal the informal expertise that Will and his staff perfected. I am sure they will do their best, and like most lovers of the Home Port, I will be back and wish them the best of luck. The Home Port tradition of unique and unforgettable dining as the sun dips slowly into the sea is truly a treasure to recall.

Aerial view of Menemsha, circa 1940

An Island Institution Is Born

The History of the Home Port

The Home Port, which is the name of the new business establishment of Capt. and Mrs. Chester Robinson at Menemsha Creek is now open and doing business. The establishment, is without a doubt, one of the most attractively situated on the Island and possesses the probabilities of becoming one of the prominent centers of summer social activities. . . . Tasteful simplicity is the keynote in finishing and furnishing of this establishment, and there is always a breeze sweeping up from the water a stone's throw away.

—The Vineyard Gazette, *June 30, 1931*

Menemsha doesn't look all that much different than it did back when Captain Chester Robinson first opened the Home Port in June 1931. It's still a sleepy little fishing village. Back then Menemsha Harbor, which opens out onto Vineyard Sound, was full of fishing boats. These days there are more yachts than fishing boats, but other than that, it's just about the same. Fishing was about all there was in Menemsha back in the '30s, so it is only fitting that a fishing boat captain be the one to open the Home Port.

For years people in Menemsha Creek—*Creek* was dropped from the village name in the late '50s—had been complaining that if they wanted to get something to eat, they had to go up to Chilmark. It wasn't far, but it wasn't right there on the water where they made their living. So Captain Robinson did something about it and went into the restaurant business. The first incarnation of the Home Port was a lunch counter, where fishermen and the few visitors from off-island could sit and have a bowl of quahog chowder and a lobster roll, or a sandwich and some ice cream, and look out over the water toward Menemsha Bight and the Elizabeth Islands from the sweeping veranda, where most people preferred to sit. Very quickly, as predicted in the article that appeared in the *Vineyard Gazette* opening week, it became "one of the prominent centers of summer social activities."

Initially, Captain Robinson wanted to call his little restaurant Chet's Place. Mrs. Robinson didn't think it was such a good idea—she preferred a nautical theme—but had she been able to see into the future, she might not have been so quick to veto her husband's suggestion, considering that two future owners of what would become one of the most popular and enduring restaurants on the Island would share her husband's first name.

Nevertheless, the restaurant was christened the Home Port, and the Home Port it has remained. The Robinsons ran their little seasonal lunch counter for six years, despite the ravages of the Great Depression and Captain Robinson's failing health.

This is where the history of the place gets a little murky. What is known is that George Hallowell purchased the Home Port from the Robinsons in 1936. Written records of the next few years have disappeared, so really all anyone has to go on are the old-timers' recollections, and those are varied and vague at best. Some say Mr. Hallowell ran the restaurant for a few years before selling it. Others say he ran it for a season and then shut the doors, and it stood, shuttered and dark, for some time. Still others say he sold it after the first year. What is known is that at some point between 1936 and 1945 the restaurant was sold to Hubert Mayhew and, under the Home Port banner, was up and running when Chester (Chet number two) Sterns bought it in September 1945. Mr. Sterns and his wife, originally from Hartford, Connecticut, were visiting friends who summered on the Island when he discovered the Home Port during a day trip to Menemsha, and he purchased the restaurant shortly thereafter. Mr. Sterns settled in nearby Chilmark and ran the Home Port for twenty-one years before selling it to Chester (Chet number three) Cummens and his wife, Esther, in 1957, though if you ask Chet Cummens, sometimes it seemed like Mr. Sterns never left. For years after Mr. Cummens had taken over, Mr. Sterns would stalk around outside the restaurant, asking exiting customers, "Was it as good as when I owned it?" I sometimes wonder if people had the heart to tell him the truth.

Chet Cummens first landed on Martha's Vineyard during World War II, stationed at the U.S. Navy radar station at Gay Head. It was while he was there that he met Esther Rabbit, whose father ran a resort in Vineyard Haven. Following his discharge, Chet and Esther were married and he went to work for his father-in-law in the resort's kitchen. After a few years working for Mr. Rabbit, Chet decided it was time to strike out on his own. At the time, there were two existing restaurants for sale on the Island—the Home Port being one of them. With his father-in-law's help, Chet bought the Home Port. I can't remember how many times Chet said over the years, "I made the right choice."

Chet was a born restaurateur. He saw right away that the Home Port was more than a lunch counter, and he went straight to work on his vision. He expanded the building, closing in the old veranda with glass and extending the kitchen, and he built a shed next to the restaurant to house two giant lobster tanks in a shared building with a bunkhouse for off-island help. Chet began evolving the menu, focusing on dinners rather than lunches, though it would be another decade before

```
                    HOME PORT
            Martha's Vineyard Island
                 Menemsha, Mass.

APPETIZERS:
        Choice of:
            Tomato or Cranberry Juice
            Quahaug Chowder
            Fresh Fruit Cup with Sherbert
SALAD:
        Tossed Salad

ENTREES:
        From our BROILER
LARGE THICK SIRLOIN STEAK             $ 4.95
TWO LOBSTERS (Our Speciality)          4.75
SINGLE LOBSTER   "    "                 3.50
NATIVE FRESH SWORDFISH                  3.00
NATIVE BAY SCALLOPS                     3.60
SALISBURY STEAK                         2.25

TWO BOILED HOT OR COLD LOBSTERS        4.75
SINGLE BOILED, as above                3.50
LOBSTER SAUTE' Meat of Two Lobsters    4.95
LOBSTER SALAD                          3.50
FRIED NATIVE BAY SCALLOPS              3.00

VEGETABLES:
        Choice of Baked or French Fries
        and Seasonal Garden Vegetables

DESSERTS:
        Dessert of the Day

BEVERAGES:
        Coffee, Tea, Sanka, Iced or Hot.
            Soda      Milk


        To Preserve the Taste and Freshness of
    our Meats and Seafoods, we prepare them only
    to Order, so PLEASE allow sufficient time in
    their preparation.

        For RESERVATION and INFORMATION
        Telephone  Mission 5-2212


            (5% Mass.Old Age Tax)
```

The Home Port menu cover and menu, circa 1950

he phased out lunch altogether. People started taking notice of what Chet was doing. Slowly the Home Port became a destination for people from across the Island, and even appeared (for the first time) in the 1961 edition of Duncan Hines's *Adventures in Good Eating,* one of the first widely published travel guides in the United States. It was the only restaurant on the Island recognized in the publication.

No one can say exactly when the Home Port became an Island institution, as it is referred to so often today, other than under Chet Cummens's stewardship. It is not something I could even imagine taking credit for. My greatest challenge over

The Home Port, 1931

these thirty-plus years has been not screwing up what Chet made so popular and did so perfectly. His cooking philosophy was simple: Serve only the freshest seafood, cooked simply, in portions that border on the outrageous. Chet was supersizing meals long before McDonald's. It was that philosophy, along with his work ethic, that made the Home Port an Island institution. I only followed his example.

Between Memorial Day and Labor Day, Chet worked like a dog. He was up at four in the morning in his bakeshop, and then he headed straight into the kitchen to begin prepping for the day. Usually around two or three, when things were all but set for the evening ahead, Chet would go up to the small apartment above the restaurant where he and Esther lived during the season for a beer and a short nap, and then he would be back down by four to oversee dinner. If he was lucky, he was in bed by eleven, only to be up long before the sun, back in the bakeshop. That was where Chet was happiest—in the bakeshop. His pies were his pride and joy.

Martha's Vineyard was still a relative secret when the Cummenses owned the Home Port. Yes, people did flock there in the summer, but it wasn't like it is today: It wasn't as country clubby, and the hills around Chilmark and Menemsha were still dotted with clapboard and Cape Cod–style houses in various stages of disrepair. The people who worked on the Island, the fishermen and store clerks, could still afford to live there and were the backbone of Chet's business. It would be another twenty years before the Island would become a playground for the rich and famous. There were, however, a few celebrities who discovered the charms of Martha's Vineyard long before it became "Hollywood East," namely James Cagney and Beverly Sills, both of whom remained loyal customers of the Home Port until their deaths.

By 1967, my first year working there, the Home Port was the Island's lobster palace, and lunch was all but an afterthought. By then a couple of other places for lunch had opened. My second season at the Home Port, lunch was eliminated altogether. We had a bonfire in the parking lot and burned all of the lunch menus. Chet sat and drank a beer and laughed. The Home Port was where people went for dinner. It was the place for fresh seafood, cooked in the Vineyard tradition, simply, which is how it has remained over these many years.

The Long Road Home

My History with the Home Port

LANDFALL

I first landed on Martha's Vineyard on July 3, 1966. To be honest, I had never even heard of Martha's Vineyard until I met John Roberts at Carson Long Military Academy in Pennsylvania. It was the summer before my senior year. John was a year behind me, and one of two students at Carson Long from the Vineyard. A freshman, Chuck Cummens, was the other. At school we all liked to talk about where we were from. Well, some people liked to talk about where they were from. There wasn't really much I could say about Granby, Connecticut, other than there was nothing there to do. I usually said I was from Hartford—people had heard of Hartford.

When John and Chuck would talk about summers on Martha's Vineyard, we would all listen with equal parts curiosity and jealousy. They talked about it like it was some magical place: warm and sunny, where there was always a party going on and the girls were all drop-dead gorgeous and scantily clad. Sometime during the dark, cold Pennsylvania winter of my junior year, after John had just finished a rather compelling story about a nighttime swim where he found himself face-to-face with a very beautiful and quite naked girl, it

was decided among a group of us that we would have to see this place with the queer name for ourselves, to see how full of it John really was.

The drive was an adventure in and of itself. My companions started out in Philadelphia before picking me up in Granby, where we continued north, a trail of empty beer cans in our wake. We caught the ferry at Woods Hole. I spent the hour-long ferry ride standing at the bow of the boat, breathing in the fresh salty air, feeling as excited as I had ever had about anything. I could not help but be taken by how beautiful, how pristine, everything was.

We found our way to John's house and, true to his word, he took us to what was, at the time anyway, the best party I had ever been to. Bright and early the next afternoon we ventured up-island to see Chuck at the Home Port and spend the afternoon at Menemsha Beach. Going to Menemsha was, like it is today, kind of like taking a step back in time. The harbor was full of fishing boats, and as we pulled into the dusty parking lot, I had my first encounter with a Cricker—that's what they call Menemsha natives—ambling toward the docks. He was a leather-skinned, salty old coot who looked at us as we piled out of the car like we were from some distant planet, mumbling something to himself I was convinced had to do with some great white whale.

Chuck's mom, Esther, greeted us at the front door of the Home Port and sat us at a table by the window. Chuck came out, still in his apron and half-soaked from his duties as dishwasher, and sat down with us. We were treated to a wonderful lunch of quahog chowder and lobster salad sandwiches as Chuck pointed out the various kinds of fish mounted on the wall. Lunch didn't last long—we were eager to beat it to the beach. Chuck was excused from his duties at the restaurant for the day, and we went out and met some people John and Chuck knew on the beach. It was a great time. That night we watched the Fourth of July fireworks in Edgartown and went to a clambake and bonfire on the beach, where I met a girl. She had dark hair and wore a blue bikini. I was doing my best to be suave and told her the little swatches of blue that covered her brought out the blue in her eyes. "My eyes are brown," she said. It didn't matter what color her eyes were—I was in paradise.

NIGHT MAN

A couple weeks before my graduation from Carson Long Military Academy, a package arrived for me. It was a large package, wrapped in brown paper. Of course, I ripped right into it. It was luggage. Nice luggage. It came with a note: "Happy Graduation. Every graduate needs luggage. USE IT! Love Mom and Dad."

I had already been accepted at the Wentworth Institute of Technology in Boston to study to be an engineer. Before the package came, I figured I would just go home to Granby and find a job for the summer and then go off to school. But somewhere along the line my sister decided she was going to come home from college for the summer. My sister and I didn't get along particularly well. We fought like cats and dogs, actually. I guess the thought of my sister and me at each other's throats all summer was more than my mother could take—hence the luggage and the subtle suggestion I spend my summer elsewhere. I was fine with that. And it got me to thinking.

On more than one occasion Chuck Cummens had talked about a few of us from Carson Long spending the summer working for his mother and father at the Home Port. It was 1967, and the Vietnam War was in full swing. Chet, Chuck's dad, had lost a few key staff members to the draft already. I wouldn't say he was desperate, but he did need a few warm bodies. My body was warm enough, I figured, so I talked to Chuck about it. I had such a wonderful time there the summer before—and that was just for a couple of beer-soaked days. I couldn't even imagine what an entire summer would be like. All it took was a call home from Chuck and I had a summer job.

The day after graduation I packed up all of my worldly possessions in my new luggage and made my way to Martha's Vineyard, settling nicely into the bunkhouse with a couple of other guys who worked there. I was given the rather dubious title of Night Man. My day started around six or seven at night, as dinner was really getting going. I was there to help out whoever needed it. I had no experience in a kitchen before my first day there, other than helping my father make a meat loaf when I was little. And I have to admit I was surprised how hectic it was, with people doing a hundred different things at once, but completely in concert. I was utterly fascinated by how it all worked. I filled a lot of cups with butter for the lobster cook and helped the dishwashers keep up; I was an extra pair of hands. One of the first things I learned was how to stay the hell out of the way.

But after dinner was when I really shined—literally. It was my job to clean up. I helped clean the kitchen and then moved into the dining room. Probably the defining task of the Night Man was cleaning the floors. The Home Port floors were a work of art. They still are. They are the original oak floors from when Chet Robinson opened back in '31. They are absolutely beautiful. At the end of every season Chet Cummens would put a new coat of polyurethane on the floors. By '67 there was probably a quarter-inch of the stuff covering the wood. They looked like a basketball court, they were so shiny. I worked late into the night making sure the floors sparkled. It was a tricky little job. Chet and Esther lived in the apartment upstairs and could hear everything that went on downstairs, so not only did I have to get the floors clean, but I had to do it making as little noise as possible.

The last thing the waitstaff did at night before they went on their merry way was stack the chairs on top of the tables so I could do the floors. By then they were eager to be done, their tips counted and their order for the package store in, and a party somewhere already in full swing. It didn't take much to upset the precarious balance of the wooden chairs on the tables, sending them crashing to the floor. It was a terrible racket, the chairs hitting the floor, and would wake up Chet and Esther. And boy, would I hear about it from Esther in the morning. "Try not to tear the entire place down," she would say.

Every morning Esther would make an inspection of my previous night's work. Most days she was pleased with everything, but when she wasn't, watch out. But she had a sense of humor, too. My first week there she called me over one afternoon and pointed to a deep scratch in the polyurethane. "What's this?" she asked. I got down on my hands and knees and looked closely at the scratch. "Looks like you didn't scrub hard enough," she said, stone-faced. At the time I had no idea she was joking. Of course, I know now it's all but impossible to scrub a scratch out of a floor with a mop. But she had me convinced I could do just that. I worked on every scratch, scrubbing and scrubbing, until I finally realized she was messing with me. But that floor sure did shine.

The worst part about the Night Man job was the fact that I worked while everyone else was out having a good time—a great time, really. Just about every night there was a party. The kitchen crew (mostly male) and the waitstaff (exclusively female back then) would go out in a group after work. Someone would make a run to the package store in Vineyard Haven (save two towns, Martha's Vineyard is dry, so acquiring beer and liquor took some planning), and everyone else would set out to the party. Usually about the time I was finishing up, the other guys who stayed in the bunkhouse would be tumbling into bed, drunk and loud, and they would be obligated to regale with the night's various debaucheries. I felt like I was missing out on something. It took a little convincing, but I finally talked Esther into letting me go out with everyone a night or two a week and finish the floors when I got back. "Don't you dare go waking us up," she warned.

I was right: I was missing out. Man, were those parties fun. We'd go out as a gang. The Home Port Gang—that's what people called us. Armed with enough alcohol to get the entire Atlantic Fleet good and drunk, we would pile into someone's car and go out to whichever beach the party was at that night. There was always a big fire and lots of girls. Hey, it was 1967. All I can say is thank God for the sexual revolution. I would do my best to drink my weight in alcohol, and then stumble back to the Home Port with everyone else and set to work on the floors. Sober, it took me a couple hours to get the 2,000 or so square feet of floor shining bright enough to pass Esther's morning inspection. Drunk, it sometimes took all night. There were a few nights when the sun was well up before I finished. I could hear the seagulls out at Lobsterville beach feeding on the incoming tide when I finally crawled into bed.

My tenure as Night Man lasted about a month. After some scandalous behavior by the lobster cook, the position came open and I was promoted. It was that first summer, cooking lobsters, I discovered I had a talent and a joy for cooking. It was hardly work at all. I remember one night thinking, I could do this for the rest of my life.

The rest, as they say, is history.

CHANGE OF PLANS

Every season I worked at the Home Port, Chet entrusted me with more and more responsibility. I made the chowder, and I could run the broilers and the fry-o-lator with my eyes closed. Chet taught me to cut the fish, although, like the baking, that was one of the things he usually did himself. With each summer working at the Home Port, I became less and less interested in becoming an engineer like I had planned and was studying to be. Initially I was going to work as an engineer until I had made enough money to buy my own restaurant. But that would take years. I didn't want to have to wait that long.

By then I was all but done with my engineering degree. I would have finished earlier, but I was in a car accident and had to skip a semester. Had that car not plowed into me, things might have been very different. With only a semester to go before graduating, I made the decision to be a chef. Well, not really be a chef as much as go into the restaurant business, with the hope of owning my own restaurant one day. It was a pretty easy decision, really. I just woke up one day and said I'm done with this. The decision was, I have to admit, made a little easier by the girl I was dating who had just broken up with me. I was heartbroken. I left school and went back to Granby with the intention of getting a job in a restaurant in Boston or one of the other big cities. I didn't even make it that far.

I was only back in Granby for a day or two when I ran into an old friend of mine, Jeff O'Donnell, the chef at a place called the Coach & Four. He happened to need a first cook. Nowadays, when everyone in a kitchen has a title, I would have been the sous-chef. But back then, I was first cook. He knew all about what I did at the Home Port.

Having worked for four summers at the Home Port, I thought I had a pretty good idea about preparing food. I learned very quickly I really only knew Home Port food. There was a whole other culinary world out there I hadn't been exposed to. Jeff was truly a talented chef. He taught me a lot about sauces and how they bring out the taste of food. At the Home Port the only sauce we ever used was butter—lots and lots and lots of butter. Enough butter to keep the dairy industry in business. Not for the faint—or weak—of heart. Jeff also taught me a lot about garnishing. To this day, I can't see a sprig of parsley without thinking of Jeff. One of the first things he taught me was how to chop parsley. You can always tell a chef's worth by how finely he or she chops parsley. He showed me how to take it off the stem and chop it up with a knife in each hand, and then put it in cheesecloth or a paper towel and wring out all of the juice, leaving wonderful dried green parsley, a method once common but hardly seen today.

I worked through the winter and the spring under Jeff, learning, before returning to the Home Port at the beginning of the summer for my fifth and final year as an employee of Chet Cummens. It didn't hurt any that I had a great time working with Jeff. If there was any doubt as to whether I was going to go into the restaurant business, that made up my mind. I knew exactly what I wanted to do. I just had to go out and do it.

But before I set out to make a name for myself in the culinary world, there was something I wanted to do. After five summers on the Vineyard, I had come to know a lot of fishermen. I admired and respected what they did. No one could tell a better story than a fisherman. The writers who frequented the Home Port usually had a hard time holding a candle to the storytelling abilities—and the stories themselves—of the fishermen I knew. After a difficult year—my first real heartbreak, dropping out of school, and the decision to plunge headlong into a career in the restaurant industry—I thought an adventure might do me some good before I went to work. After hearing all of the stories told by the fishermen, I decided I would make some of my own. When the season closed at the Home Port, I got in my car and drove across the country to San Diego with the idea of finding work on a tuna fishing boat.

I have to admit I didn't know crap about tuna fishing. But if I had a nickel for every time one of those salty old bastards fresh off a fishing boat would say, "If there's one thing every fishing boat needs, it's someone who can cook," I would have owned my own restaurant by then. I heard stories about how guys would choose which boat to work on based on how good the cook was. I knew I pretty much had that part covered. And I was a hard worker, with a broad set of shoulders, and I knew how to tie knots and straighten lines, so I figured I would be of enough use to land myself a job on a boat. Boy, was I wrong.

I tried boat after boat, but it turned out I couldn't get a job on a boat to save my life. "Sorry, kid. We just don't need anybody," they all said. After trying about fifty boats, I realized there might be a problem—quite a problem, actually. Apparently there was something of a dispute as to where Chilean territorial waters ended and international waters began. As a result, the Chilean navy was seizing any American fishing boat that was even close. That was where the fishing grounds were. Captains and boat owners didn't want their boats seized, so they all decided to sit that season out while the politicians from both countries figured everything out. Seeing as I had never been to California, however, I made the best of it, seeing what there was to see, visiting my crazy (in a good way) uncle Bill, his lovely wife Ruth, and my cousins Kim, Bill Jr., and Craig, and generally just bumming around until I ran out of money.

COMPANY MAN

After my somewhat disappointing adventure out West, I went back to Boston to find a job. It took less than a week. I saw a classified ad in the paper for Valle's Steak House. Back in the '70s and early '80s, Valle's was a pretty big player in the Northeast. I showed up for an interview at the Newton, Massachusetts, store and was interviewed

The East's Most popular and well known Restaurants

A postcard from Valle's Steak house, "the East's most popular and well known restaurants"

the novelty of the place wore off. This was 1972, and Atlanta wasn't as cosmopolitan as it is today. It was still very Southern. The idea of a Northeastern steak house really didn't excite the people there. I can't tell you how many times people would ask, "Where's the fried chicken? Where's the mac and cheese? Where are the collard greens?" This is what people wanted down there. They had no interest in Yankee pot roast.

The Atlanta store was also one of the few Valle's that served breakfast. As assistant manager, it was my job to open the restaurant every morning. Breakfast was, at best, sporadic. Lunch and dinner weren't much better. Some mornings ten people would walk through the door; other days we would be slammed. I had no idea how to prepare for each morning because I had no idea how busy we would be from one day to the next. It led to a certain amount of creativity in the kitchen. Instead of preparing twenty pounds of home fries and bacon and sausage each morning, which, more often than not, would just get thrown away, I started dropping everything but the grits and the eggs into the fry-o-lator. It wasn't like I was

by a little bald-headed man in a cheap black suit and saggy white socks. He introduced himself as Donald. I didn't think much of it at the time, figuring he was just a midlevel manager weeding out applicants. He hired me on the spot and told me to show up to start my training the next day. Turns out the man who hired me was Donald Valle himself.

Training at Valle's was like going through boot camp but without all the push-ups. It lasted six months. During that time they worked you like a rented mule. Not many trainees actually finished. You had to know the restaurant inside and out.

After I completed my training, I was offered an assistant manager's position in a brand-new Valle's in Atlanta. But Atlanta didn't turn out to be the market they thought it would be. After a few weeks, frying the hell out of everything—it just got the food started so I could finish it on the grill. This was by no means anything new. It's a fairly common practice in the restaurant business, though generally frowned upon. We did it out of necessity, more than anything. I was saving the restaurant a lot of money. It was a practice I taught every cook I hired, though most of them were already quite familiar with it.

After a few floundering months, Arthur Hanson, the senior vice president of Valle's, showed up unannounced in Atlanta to see for himself why our numbers were so bad. He had been there for a couple of days, chewing everyone out, trying to figure what we were doing wrong. On Sunday (the only day I didn't have to open the restaurant), as soon as I was in the door, the breakfast cook—probably the sixth or seventh we had gone through by then—pulled me aside and said, "Mr. Hanson came in earlier. We were pretty busy, so he put on an apron and helped me out." "Good," I said. "No," the cook replied, a horrified look on his face. "Not good at all. I had everything but the scrambled eggs in the fryer. Mr. Hanson lost it. He wants to see you." I went into the office, where Mr. Hanson was on the phone with Mr. Valle. He started talking to both of us at the same time. "We have the cooks railroading food," Hanson told Valle, but looking at me when he said it. "I don't see what we are paying these assistant managers all this money for. Obviously, he's not doing his job."

I could not believe what I was hearing. I was absolutely crushed. I was working my ass off for them. I was on salary, making about $250 a week, which wasn't bad money back then, except for the fact I was working ninety-plus-hour weeks, essentially working two jobs. He knew that, too. Even though we were on salary, we still punched time cards. "I'll tell you what, Mr. Hanson," I said. Hanson held out the phone so Valle could hear what I was saying. "Starting next week, you train the breakfast cooks and see how it all works. I'm done here." He looked at me for a second, and Valle said something. "I think he just quit," Hanson told Valle. "I don't care. He can leave right now," Hanson said, I think more to me than Valle.

I turned and started out the door, stopped and threw Hanson my keys, then went out and drove over to my apartment and called Mr. Valle. He took my call right away. "Will, you need to go back and apologize to Mr. Hanson," Valle said. "I'm sorry, Mr. Valle, but if anyone needs to apologize, it's Mr. Hanson. You have no idea what it's like down here. You have no idea how hard I've worked for you." "Yes. Yes I do, Will," Valle said. "Don't be foolish. We can make this work. Don't be foolish now." I replied, "No, Mr. Valle. I quit, and I need to stay quit." Valle said, "Tell you what. My nephew runs the Springfield store. I'll bring you home. You can come home and work with him. It's a great house. A busy house. Don't be foolish." "No," I told him, "I think it's foolish to stay."

Years later I ran into Arthur Hanson again. Mr. Valle had died, and with him went his empire. There were only a few Valle's left, all in New England. I was on my way from the Vineyard to my house in Maine with my daughter and stepdaughter when I saw a Valle's sign. We hadn't had lunch yet, so I stopped. And what do you know, there's Mr. Hanson standing at the podium. As he was seating us, I said, "You probably won't remember me, but I worked for you about ten years back." I told him my name. It didn't ring a bell, at least not right away. We sat down and ordered and were enjoying our meal when he came walking toward me wagging his finger, a big smile on his face. "I do remember you," he said. We talked for a while. It was all water under the bridge.

LANDMARK LESSONS

In the late 1970s Anthony's Pier 4 in Boston was one of the premier restaurants in the country, if not the world. It still is, for that matter, though since the advent of celebrity chefs, its popularity has waned some. The restaurant itself is a landmark, overlooking Boston Harbor, with floor-to-ceiling windows on three sides of the dining room providing commanding views of the city skyline, Logan Airport, and the water with its passing ships. Part of owner Anthony Athanas's brilliance as a restaurateur was his showmanship. He was a diminutive man, immaculately groomed and impeccably dressed. There is a story that after Elizabeth Taylor commented on how much she liked a double-breasted, pearl-buttoned sport coat he had on one night when she came in to eat, he went out and had eight more tailored just like it.

As soon as you walk into Pier 4, you know this is the place to be. The foyer walls are covered with pictures of Mr. Athanas with actors and politicians, professional athletes and writers, journalists and television personalities. The restaurant is massive: two kitchens and seating for more than 800. It was Mr. Athanas's flagship restaurant. He had three others when I started working for him: Anthony's Hawthorne, Hawthorne by the Sea, and the General Glover House. All were incredibly successful, though nothing like Pier 4. Working for Anthony Athanas was like working for Emeril Lagasse or Wolfgang Puck in their heyday. He was larger than life. Everything he touched instantly turned to gold. The many lessons he taught me without even knowing it were invaluable.

With my Valle's experience under my belt, I returned to Boston to find my next great culinary adventure. Pier 4 was the first place I applied. It was the only place I applied. Going in, I knew I wouldn't have to settle for the first job I could find. I didn't have to be a pot washer or a line cook somewhere. And it didn't hurt any that I knew seafood inside out. Looking back at it now, I can't believe I put all of my eggs in that one basket the way I did. When I went in for my first interview, as I stood in the foyer and looked at the pictures of Mr. Athanas with Judy Garland and Joe DiMaggio and Johnny Carson, I truly believed I had something to offer Mr. Athanas. I just thank God he did, too.

I was hired as the kitchen steward, which basically put me in charge of the front of the kitchen. Mr. Athanas wanted the chef to concentrate on the cooking. Chefs working for Mr. Athanas had very little wiggle room when it came to their cooking. He designed the menu and expected his chefs to produce it to the letter, just as he intended. And if there was one thing you did not want to do, that was do anything to displease Mr. Athanas. He had a reputation as being a hard man to work for, an incredibly demanding employer. He was. But he was also incredibly fair, and he generously rewarded those who worked hard for him.

The volume Pier 4 did was tremendous. There would be 500 people in the dining rooms and two weddings going on at the same time. It was my job to anticipate anything that could go wrong in the kitchen and fix it before it happened. If they

A postcard from the world-famous Anthony's Pier 4

needed lemons cut or coffee brewed, I made sure it happened. I was the go-between for the waitstaff and the various cooks. I looked at each plate as it came out and communicated any problems I saw with the chef. I learned an incredible amount about food in a very short period of time. Mr. Athanas would call me up to his office and ask me what I saw in the kitchen. I was his eyes and ears. When there was a problem in the dining room with the food, a steak was overcooked or something was wrong, I was the one who went out and took care of it. Mr. Athanas wanted his chef in the kitchen, cooking. He had me wear a shirt and tie, a long white coat, and white buck shoes. He wanted someone with a professional demeanor going out to resolve any issues the customers had. Whatever needed to be done, I did it. If the dishwasher was backed up, I rolled up my sleeves and jumped right in. I washed a lot of dishes. I used to joke that I was the highest paid dishwasher in the city of Boston. It was an absolutely wonderful job. I loved just about every minute of it.

Getting a reservation at Pier 4 was about as easy as getting an audience with the Pope. Most people didn't get a reservation. They came in and put their name down and waited. And waited. And waited. But that was all part of the Pier 4 experience. Of course, exceptions were made. I wish I could name all of the celebrities who came in while I was there. Mr. Athanas knew how to treat them. He understood that celebrities added to the cachet of the restaurant. Just about every night someone of note was at Pier 4.

Mr. Athanas liked to throw parties for his friends, particularly his famous friends. One year he had a party for legendary Boston Pops conductor Arthur Fiedler's eightieth birthday. Now I've seen some good parties over the years, but this one topped them all. I'll just say that the Beluga caviar wasn't the most extravagant thing there that night.

Mr. Athanas didn't take any crap either—from anyone. I will never forget a conversation with a customer I had the pleasure of overhearing. It was late in the evening and the kitchen was about out of baked potatoes. I went out to the maître d' podium to see how many people were waiting to be seated so I could gauge how many more potatoes needed to be cooked. This was before microwaves were widely used, so it took some time to bake the potatoes. That night Mr. Athanas happened to be at the podium. The man was omnipresent at the restaurant. He was the first in and the last to leave. As I came up to the podium, I saw a little old woman giving Mr. Athanas quite a dressing down.

"This place is just a tourist trap," she said quite loudly, poking a bony finger in his face. "The food isn't even that great." Mr. Athanas just stood and looked at her with a slight smile on his face, as suave and cool as ever. When she finished he looked her right in the eye, smiled, and, as if he were discussing the weather on a particularly pleasant day, said, "Yes, ma'am, you're absolutely right. Now get the hell out of my restaurant." The look on the old woman's face was priceless. She was absolutely floored. Speechless, she turned and stormed back out to the tour bus she came in on. Mr. Athanas just shook his head and smiled his sly little smile at me. Over the years I have had identical conversations with customers at the Home Port. The reality of the restaurant business is you can't please everyone. Every time I would tell someone, as pleasantly as possible, to get the hell out of my restaurant, I would think of Mr. Athanas.

But Pier 4 was far from a tourist trap. It was an incredible restaurant. Locals went there. It was the place to go and be seen and celebrate. It did draw a lot of tourists, but that's because the experience they had at Pier 4 was second to none. If you came to town and asked for a dinner recommendation, it was the first place everyone sent you. Mr. Athanas saw to that. It was all part of his genius. He invited taxi drivers inside the restaurant and fed them, and set up a coffee stand outside, so it was the first place any cabbie would recommend.

Anthony Athanas died in 2005 from complications of Alzheimer's disease. He was ninety-three. In his obituary, Boston mayor Thomas M. Menino called him "Boston's host. . . . Pier 4 with Anthony Athanas at the door was the place to be, always alive, and always full of people." Along with Chet Cummens, Mr. Athanas was one of the biggest influences in my life. Hardly a day goes by when I don't think about him. I could never thank him enough for all he did for me.

CLOSER TO HOME

The scuttlebutt about a new restaurant started about the same time I started at Pier 4. A year and a half later, it was a reality. The Cummaquid Inn on Cape Cod was Mr. Athanas's final restaurant in his empire. A few weeks before the opening of the Cummaquid, I was asked to go down and help out opening weekend. There were more than 700 people working for Mr. Athanas at the time, so I considered it quite an honor.

The setup of the Cummaquid was fantastic. Like all of Mr. Athanas's restaurants, everything was done first class. Opening night was huge. After the last customer had gone, they had a little party for the staff. Mr. Athanas, his wife, and sons; Chet Watson, Mr. Athanas's brother-in-law and general manager of the new restaurant; and some other members of the family sat at one table and the employees all sat at another table. We were all celebrating what everyone knew was a very successful opening. We decided to buy Mr. Athanas a really good bottle of champagne, and someone at our table made a toast: "To Mr. Athanas, congratulations on the successful opening of another great restaurant. Here's to your success." Mr. Athanas smiled and raised his glass, and said, "Well it damn well better be a successful opening. I have enough people here to run two goddamn restaurants." That's how Mr. Athanas was.

I was originally supposed to work at the Cummaquid Inn for opening weekend and then go back to my duties at Pier 4. But when they saw how busy they were going to be—far beyond their already high expectations—it was decided to keep me there for the entire week. Then two weeks. Then a month. Then permanently.

The menu from Anthony's Cummaquid Inn

The chef at the Cummaquid was straight out of the Culinary Institute of America. He only lasted about a month. We had been incredibly busy. We were in the kitchen prepping for dinner when he came through the kitchen from his room upstairs carrying a big laundry bag and went out the back door without saying a word to anyone. It was his first day off in a couple of weeks, and we all just figured he was going to do his laundry. That was the last I ever saw of him. The next day I took over cooking duties at the Cummaquid.

The first summer at the Cummaquid was insane. Three weeks in a row, I clocked more than a hundred hours a week. I didn't mind it at all, though—I enjoyed the work. They put us up in the inn, so I was right there. I would get up early in the morning and go downstairs and work straight through until two or three the next morning, then go to my room and crawl into bed, exhausted, sleep for a few hours, and do it all over again. My mother came to visit me and said I looked like hell. I weighed less than I did when I was in high school. I didn't feel like hell, though. I felt as good as I had ever felt in my life. One of Mr. Athanas's other chefs was complaining about the hours he was working. It was something paltry, like sixty hours a week. Mr. Athanas showed him my time card and said, "I don't want to hear it."

Things slowed down considerably in the fall. The Cummaquid was still very popular, but it wasn't like it was when it first opened. I had gone and gotten myself married. I couldn't spend every waking moment working. My life had changed, and I had to think about the future. I knew I would never be anything more than an employee for the Athanases. It was a family-run business, and as trusted and valuable as I was, I wasn't family. Back when I was at Pier 4, Jim Sobel, the purchaser for the restaurant, and I were talking one afternoon. Jim was as high up as anyone not in the family was ever going to get in the company. He gave me a great piece of advice about working for the Athanas family: "Do your job every day like you own the place. Don't go changing stuff, don't get too creative, just do the best job you can and always be trying to improve things without stepping over the line." But I was moving past that point now, and all the time I still had it in the back of my mind that I wanted to open a place of my own. By then I knew I had what it took to make a go of it. A few years back I had set a goal for myself that I would own my own restaurant by the time I was twenty-seven. Well, I was twenty-seven, and it seemed like owning my own restaurant was a million miles away.

HOME AGAIN

I was crawling into bed late one night when my wife said, "Chet Cummens called. He wants you to call him back immediately." My first thought was that something was wrong: Someone was sick, or worse. I called him in Florida the first thing the next morning. We talked for a few minutes and I hung up the phone, stunned. It took me a moment to collect myself. "What's wrong?" my wife asked. "Nothing," I said. "Chet wants me to buy the Home Port."

The Cummenses were like a second family to me. Even after I stopped working at the Home Port, I kept in pretty close touch with them. I

would go see them on the Vineyard when I could. Esther liked to approve, or disapprove, of the girls I dated. I took the ones I knew she would like to see.

During our phone conversation, Chet said over and over he wanted me to own the Home Port. Chet's son, Chuck, had no interest in running it. He wanted to do something else. "I want to keep it in the family," Chet said. He was very proud of the business he had built. He wanted it to carry on, his business, his vision of what it should be, and I think he knew if someone else bought it, things would change too much.

It was the opportunity of a lifetime. Ten lifetimes. There was only one problem: money.

I was making good money at the Cummaquid. But with a wife, a baby on the way, a car payment, and rent, there wasn't much left. We had a couple thousand dollars in the bank, but that was about it. I called my mother to tell her. "Don't we have a rich uncle or something I don't know about?" I asked, already knowing the answer but still hopeful.

I called my friend Kenny Kidd. He was about the smartest person I knew. If anyone could help me figure out how to come up with a quarter of a million dollars, it would be my buddy Ken. I knew Ken from when I worked at the Home Port. His family had a summer house on the Vineyard. Though he never actually worked at the Home Port, he was always part of our gang. From an early age, Ken was making money. He had his own lawn-mowing business at fourteen. When I called him for help, he was already the vice president of a bank in Worcester. "We'll figure this out," he promised.

Kenny went with me to meet with Chet and his accountant, and we figured out everything I had to do, all of the business plans and projections and everything else a bank would need to give me a loan. They may as well have been speaking Russian as far as I was concerned. Kenny helped me get it all set up, all of the documents and every-thing. "You need to do something about that bank account," he said. My father-in-law helped me out with that one. He didn't have the money to lend me, so he took out a personal loan and dumped about twenty grand into my savings account so it looked like I had a little money saved.

Our first stop was Martha's Vineyard National Bank. Kenny and I had a meeting with Bill Honey, the bank president. Ken walked in with me in his three-piece suit, and he and Mr. Honey started talking about banking. I was just sitting there lis-tening to them go on and on about something I had no idea about, when Ken leaned over and pounded his fist on Mr. Honey's desk. "This is a Vineyard business!" Kenny shouted. "This should be done on the Island with a Vineyard bank. If you don't want to do it, my bank in Worcester will. But it should be here. This should be done here." My jaw hit the floor. When Kenny finished with his

little tirade, Mr. Honey thanked us and said the matter would be discussed at the next committee meeting.

A month went by with no word. Ken told me not to worry. Then another month passed. Ken said maybe I should start worrying a little. "But they haven't told you no yet," he added. The Cummenses had wanted to close the deal in January. It was already the end of January, and I was a long way from having anything. Chet said he would wait until I had an answer, either way. "I want you to have the Home Port," he repeated. But I wasn't the only person who wanted the Home Port. A couple from New Jersey was very eager to own the restaurant—and they could afford it. I couldn't make Chet and Esther wait forever. I was beginning to get a little desperate.

I called Dave Flanders, the real estate agent who was handling the Home Port sale. Dave was a local guy, from Chilmark, and an incredibly nice man, known and loved by all. I had met him many, many times over the years working at the Home Port. I decided to call him. "It's my understanding someone from New Jersey wants to buy the Home Port," I said. "As you probably know, I'm trying to raise the money to buy it myself. I spoke with Mr. Honey a few months ago but I haven't heard back from him, so I'm assuming that's dead. I just want you to know, and maybe you could pass it along, that I would really be interested in running the

BYOB

People sometimes find it hard to believe that the Home Port doesn't serve alcohol. No wine. No beer. Nothing. Nada. Zilch. It never has. I couldn't even if I wanted to. That is one of the many quirks—some say charming, some say inconvenient—of Martha's Vineyard. Of the six towns on the Island, four of them are bone dry. The only two municipalities that allow the sale of alcohol are Oak Bluffs and Edgartown. For people anywhere else on the Island, running to the package store is more than just a trip down the street.

Not that I'm complaining.

Being unable to serve alcohol means more tables in the dining room because I don't have to have a bar. There isn't the headache of locking it up every night, or the liability of serving alcohol on the premises. It's not like customers can't have a glass of wine with their meal or a cocktail while they wait for their table at the raw bar, however. They just have to bring it with them.

Most people who spend any time on the Vineyard have come to terms with this little technicality. In fact, many embrace it. The last time I can even remember the town of Chilmark (the municipality that governs the village of Menemsha) discussing repealing its blue laws was in the late '60s. People, I have found, enjoy bringing their own drinks to a restaurant. Not only are they saving a lot of money (not that saving a few bucks is a major concern for most visitors to Martha's Vineyard), as most restaurants mark up alcohol at least 100 percent, but they get to drink exactly what they want with their dinner. If they want a special wine not found on most wine lists, they can drink that wine; if they want to drink a beer only found on the West Coast, they can drink that beer. And if they want to drink 180-proof grain alcohol, we help them up from under the table and put them in a cab—I speak of that from experience.

Bringing your own alcoholic beverages also affords people a certain amount of creativity they would not otherwise have when it comes to drinks in a restaurant. I've seen kegs of beer wheeled in on a dolly and put under the table, fully stocked bars packed neatly in a cooler, purses full of the mini bottles you get on an airplane, and everything from thousand-dollar bottles of wine to Two-Buck Chuck.

Of course, we help out customers when it comes to fixing their drinks. We provide most any setup anyone could possibly want. We have chilled marble wine coolers and ice buckets for champagne drinkers, and we'll even open the bottle of wine at no charge. That wasn't always the case, but I could not see charging for such a simple and necessary service. I felt downright guilty actually, charging someone to open a bottle of wine they brought because they had to.

kitchen for the new owners. If I can't get it myself, running it would be the next best thing."

Dave was quiet for a moment. "You know, Will, I'm on the board of directors at Martha's Vineyard National Bank. I had no idea you were interested in buying the Home Port. To be honest, it hasn't come up in a committee meeting. I'll make sure it is discussed this month."

A couple weeks later I got a letter from the bank approving my loan. The Home Port was mine. I called Kenny to tell him the good news. The following week a letter from him came in the mail:

Will,
Congratulations! M.V. Natl Bank is insane to support you. I mean, really . . . who would give you a loan to finance a $275,000 purchase of a restaurant with only a 3 percent down payment. You must have a damn good financial adviser is all I can say.

I am very pleased to see you take over the Home Port, and I wish you every success in the future. Who knows, I may even eat there this summer after going to the Island for 29 years—After all the Galley just isn't what it used to be—Red is getting along in years. . . .

I could hear him laughing as he wrote it.

Ken died of cancer a few years later. Eighteen years after his death, Kenny's son, Jessie, came to work for me. I told Jessie many times how much his father meant to me. On his last day working at the Home Port, I gave him the letter his father wrote me.

Kenny Kidd (at left) hanging out at the Home Port bunk house, 1970

ODE TO THE HOME PORT

By April Night

As we wait to hear the fate,
do not dismiss the past
a place where hungry summer folks
got their dinners fast.

From Chet to Will
it was the deal good eats would still remain,
where Cobalt Blue and fantastic views kept them
    coming back.

They came to eat,
we worked to seat
paying college bills
while single moms served all night long to clothe their
    little feet.

It wasn't just a "spot" for us,
but a place to work with friends
from slime pond dips to 10 percent tips
we knew we'd have a laugh.

Sizzling sautés on heavy trays
and wet spots on the floor,
we made it through and so will you, in spirit that's
    for sure.
Oh Home Port you were good to us, except for back
    door lines.

BDS kept cooks afloat while tips kept front staff smiling.
All the while bus buckets kept on a piling.

Goodbye old girl and thanks, your legacy will remain.
A place where families loved, workers laughed,
    Holthams lived; we loved you all the same.

For some you gave us love and others gave us fame
but what we all learned from you is, hard work will pave
    the way.

Lobster bisque (p. 32)

For Starters

Manhattan Clam Chowder

Quahog Chowder

Fish Chowder

Seafood Chowder

Lobster Bisque

Shrimp Bisque

Mussel Soup

Lobster Stew

Oyster Stew

Seafood Stew

Littlenecks on the Half Shell

Stuffed Quahogs

Clams Casino

Clam Fritters

Steamed Clams

Steamed Mussels

Oysters on the Half Shell

Stuffed Oysters

Oysters Casino

Oysters with Ginger Saffron Sauce

Oysters Rockefeller

Oyster Fritters

Lobster Cocktail

Lobster Cakes

Lobster-Stuffed Deviled Eggs

Shrimp Cocktail

Shrimp Scampi

Ham-Wrapped Shrimp

Shrimp Jalapeño

Broiled Scallops

Smoked Scallops

Scallops Ceviche

Green Scallops

Scallops Casino

Smoked Bluefish Pâté

Smoked Fish Dip

Smoked Marlin

Codfish Cakes

Tuna Tartare

Crab Salad Lettuce Roll-Ups

Crab Cakes

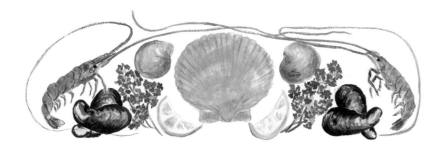

For Starters

CHOWDERS

Chowder—or chowda, as we New Englanders call it—has long been a part of our culture, so much so that Herman Melville devoted an entire chapter (chapter 15) to it in *Moby Dick*. The first chowders were made by hungry settlers more than 300 years ago and consisted of foodstuffs they had on hand: clams, fish, lobster, scallops, shrimp, oysters, eels, chicken, beef, corn—whatever they could get their hands on. More often than not, it wasn't much. Those sparse ingredients were added to bread (usually stale scraps), wild onions, salt pork when available (to enhance the flavor), and milk—the one constant ingredient in New England chowder. In other parts of the country, tomatoes were, and still are, used instead of milk. It was all combined in an iron pot to simmer over the fire and, as it's called, build.

Early Martha's Vineyard chowders consisted largely of corn, the dietary staple during the bleak winter months, and had a thin, gruel-like consistency. A thinner consistency than the paste-like mainland chowders remains a Vineyard chowder trademark today. Around the mid-1600s potatoes arrived in greater numbers by trade ships, creating the modern chowders we now know and love. Modern Martha's Vineyard chowders are distinguished by the use of the quahog, as opposed to the sea clams used in most mainland chowders.

Manhattan Clam Chowder

Did I serve Manhattan clam chowder at the Home Port? No. I would have been run out of town on a rail. But that doesn't mean I don't love it as an alternative to the traditional cream-based New England chowders. The fact that it takes about half the time to build doesn't hurt any either. For a little extra flavor, use quahogs along with the sea clams in this recipe.

1. Melt butter in a 4-quart heavy-bottomed pot. Add onions, green peppers, carrots, garlic, and celery and cook over medium heat for 5 minutes, stirring frequently. Be careful not to burn the garlic.
2. Add the remaining ingredients (except parsley) and continue to cook over medium heat until potatoes are tender but not soft.
3. Serve topped with a little fresh parsley.

SERVES 8–10

3 tablespoons butter

1½ cups chopped onion, cut into ½-inch pieces

½ cup chopped green pepper, cut into ¼-inch pieces

2 carrots, peeled and chopped into ¼-inch pieces

2 garlic cloves, chopped

1 celery stalk, chopped into ¼-inch pieces

4 pints sea clams (fresh if possible), minced

1 (28-ounce) can diced tomatoes

3 medium potatoes, chopped into ½- to ¾-inch pieces

4 9-ounce bottles (36 ounces) clam juice

1 teaspoon basil

1 teaspoon marjoram

2 dashes Tabasco

4 dashes Worcestershire sauce

Salt and pepper to taste

Chopped fresh parsley for garnish

Quahog Chowder

This is the same chowder I served at the Home Port. It's a recipe I'm quite proud of, naturally, considering it is one of my signature recipes and has been named "Best Chowder" in numerous publications and contests over the years.

Not long after I bought the Home Port, I was invited to attend a wedding of some friends. There was a handwritten note attached to the invitation: "We don't want a present, just a batch of your wonderful chowder." Naturally, I complied. How could you deny any bride's request on her wedding day? It became a tradition. A batch of chowder always accompanied me to celebratory events—and events not so celebratory in nature. Instead of flowers, I began sending families mourning the deaths of loved ones a batch of chowder—the quintessential comfort food on the Vineyard.

At the Home Port, every batch of chowder was made from scratch. Each batch started by steaming six bushels of quahogs. Whenever possible, steam the quahogs open. This creates a wonderful broth that can be used as the base of the chowder. Shucking them is another option, but you don't get as much broth. When fresh quahogs aren't available, frozen ones will work nicely. I also use sea clams in my chowder. The sweetness of the sea clams mellows the flavor just enough while keeping the chowder good and meaty. When cooking at home, experiment a little. It all comes down to personal taste. However, the general consensus is there has to be more than 50 percent quahog meat in it to call it quahog chowder.

20 large quahogs

¼ pound butter

¾ cup chopped onion

½ cup chopped celery

2 garlic cloves, chopped

1 tablespoon chopped fresh dill

½ teaspoon dried thyme

½ teaspoon black pepper

1 dash Tabasco

2 dashes Worcestershire sauce

3 tablespoons flour

2 pints sea clams, chopped

1 quart clam broth (page 183)

4 or 5 large potatoes, peeled and diced

1 quart heavy cream

1. Steam open quahogs in 1 pint of water. Be sure to save the broth. Remove quahogs from shells and chop into ½-inch pieces.
2. Melt butter in a heavy soup kettle or Dutch oven. Add onions, celery, garlic, dill, thyme, black pepper, Tabasco, and Worcestershire sauce. Sauté on medium heat for 5–6 minutes.
3. Add flour and continue cooking for another 4 minutes over low heat, stirring occasionally.
4. Add quahogs, clams, and broth and bring to a boil.
5. Add potatoes and boil on medium heat until potatoes are tender.
6. Warm heavy cream and stir into chowder. Let stand for 2 hours.
7. Reheat before serving. (Do not boil.) Serve with oyster crackers.

SERVES 8–10

Options: Add a little bacon or salt pork to fortify the flavor.

Fish Chowder

6 tablespoons butter

1½ cups chopped onion, cut into ½-inch pieces

¾ cup chopped celery, cut into ¼-inch pieces

2 garlic cloves, chopped

3 tablespoons flour

⅛ teaspoon dry thyme

¼ teaspoon dry dill

4 bay leaves

1 tablespoon parsley flakes

3–4 dashes Tabasco

5–6 dashes Worcestershire sauce

4 cups fish stock (page 180)

3 cups chopped potatoes, peeled and cut into ½- to ¾-inch pieces

3 pounds fish, boneless and skinless, cut into 2-inch pieces

3 cups heavy cream

Salt and pepper to taste

Second only to quahog chowder in my book, this recipe makes a wonderful appetizer or main course on a cold day. Use only fish with firm flesh like monkfish, halibut, swordfish, cod, or salmon. I prefer a combination of several different types of fish, but I always make sure to include salmon to provide some color.

1. Melt butter in a 4-quart heavy-bottomed pot. Add onions, celery, and garlic and cook over medium heat for 6 minutes. Stir frequently so garlic doesn't burn.

2. Add flour, thyme, dill, bay leaves, parsley, Tabasco, and Worcestershire sauce and cook over medium-low heat for 5 minutes.

3. Add fish stock and bring to a boil.

4. Add potatoes and keep at a slow boil for 15 minutes. Stir often.

5. Add fish and heavy cream and let simmer for 15–20 minutes. When fish reaches desired doneness, add salt and pepper to taste.

SERVES 8–10

Options: Use salt pork or bacon instead of butter for a little extra flavor.

Seafood Chowder

Another great chowder for a frosty day anywhere you happen to be. Feel free to mix and match different fish and other seafood ingredients, depending on what's freshest and what you like. I recommend salmon, but any fish with a firm texture (like halibut, bass, or swordfish) will work great. Make enough for left-overs. This chowder is fantastic fresh out of the pot but even better the next day.

1. Melt butter in a 4-quart heavy-bottomed pot. Add onions, celery, and garlic and cook over medium heat for 5 minutes. Stir frequently so garlic does not burn.
2. Add flour, thyme, dill, white pepper, Tabasco, and Worcestershire sauce and cook over medium-low heat for 5 minutes, stirring frequently.
3. Add clam broth or fish stock and vegetable juice and bring to a boil.
4. Add potatoes and keep at a slow boil for 15 minutes, stirring frequently.
5. Add scallops, shrimp, and fish and simmer for 10 minutes.
6. Add lobster meat, mussels, littlenecks, and heavy cream and simmer for 10–12 minutes.
7. Add salt and pepper to taste and serve. When reheating, do it slowly.

SERVES 8–10

8 tablespoons butter

1 cup chopped onion, cut into ¼-inch pieces

1 cup chopped celery, cut into ¼-inch pieces

2 garlic cloves, minced

6 tablespoons flour

⅛ teaspoon thyme

¼ teaspoon dry dill

¼ teaspoon white pepper

4 drops Tabasco

6 drops Worcestershire sauce

4 cups clam broth (page 183) or fish stock (page 180)

1 cup vegetable juice, such as V-8

4 cups chopped red potatoes, skin on, cut into ½- to ¾-inch pieces

½ pound scallops

½ pound shrimp, peeled, deveined, and chopped into bite-size pieces

2 pounds salmon or firm whitefish

½ pound lobster meat

24 mussels, steamed and picked (save the broth)

24 littleneck clams, steamed and picked (save the broth)

1 quart heavy cream

Salt and pepper to taste

Bisques

Lobster Bisque

¼ cup extra-virgin olive oil

1½ cups chopped onion

1 cup chopped celery

1 cup chopped carrots

2 garlic cloves, minced

8–10 lobster bodies

¼ cup brandy

¼ teaspoon thyme

4 bay leaves

½ teaspoon Old Bay or preferred seafood spice

1 tablespoon paprika

1 quart water

1 cup vegetable juice, such as V-8

2 tablespoons lobster base

2 cups heavy cream

¼ cup dry sherry

4 tablespoons butter

2 tablespoons flour

1 pound lobster meat

Salt and pepper to taste

It's the age-old question: Is bisque really bisque if there is meat in it? Well, as far as I'm concerned, yes. Really, is anyone going to complain if there are wonderful chunks of lobster in bisque? My bisques always have meat in them, and in more than thirty years, I haven't received one complaint yet.

For this bisque, I use the bodies of lobsters, which have some meat in them, especially females if they have eggs. The tamale (liver) has lots of flavor and can be used, but it has a tendency to turn bitter if overcooked. At the Home Port we cook and pick between fifty and a hundred lobsters each day, leaving plenty of lobster bodies for this stock. Remember, the lobster bodies need to be broken down. First, remove the stomach sack and then chop the body into pieces.

1. Heat olive oil in a large heavy-bottomed pan over medium heat. Add onion, celery, and carrots and cook for 3–4 minutes.
2. Add garlic and chopped lobster bodies and cook for 10 minutes.
3. Remove pan from heat and flambé with brandy. (Be careful.) After the flame dies down, add thyme, bay leaves, Old Bay, paprika, and water and bring to a boil. Reduce heat and simmer for 30 minutes.
4. Strain through a fine-mesh strainer and return liquid to pot.
5. Add vegetable juice, lobster base, heavy cream, and sherry and continue to simmer.
6. Meanwhile, in a separate saucepan, make a roux: Melt butter, add flour, and cook over medium heat for 5 minutes. Stir frequently so the roux does not burn.
7. Pour roux into main pot and bring to a boil. Reduce heat and simmer for 5 minutes.
8. Add lobster meat and salt and pepper to taste.
9. Serve in warm bowls.

SERVES 8–10

And That's the Way It Is

"Who is your favorite celebrity customer?"

It's a question I am frequently asked. And it's a tough question to answer because, over the years, a lot of famous people have eaten at the Home Port, many of whom I have had the pleasure to get to know on a personal level. James Cagney is on my list, because he was really the first famous person I saw there. He was eating at the Home Port before the rich and famous had really discovered Martha's Vineyard. Then there's Beverly Sills, because she was a wonderful woman and a loyal customer. Michael J. Fox, well, he's a good friend and funny as hell. And I can't forget Linda Fairstein: She does put the Home Port in her books, after all. But if I have to declare one celebrity above all others as my favorite, it would have to be Walter Cronkite. And I don't think there is anyone who could fault me for that. The man was an American icon—someone I grew up watching on television every night. He was Uncle Walter.

After he retired from CBS, Walter and his wife, Betsy, were regular fixtures on the Island. They had a nice little house in Edgartown. He was an avid sailor and was very active in several of the Island's philanthropic organizations. He was an incredibly nice, likeable man—grandfatherly, even. You almost wanted to jump in his lap and ask him to tell you a story. I can only imagine some of the stories he could tell.

Walter insisted we call him by his first name. He made it a point to talk to people when they approached him. Talking to him, it was easy to forget he was one of the most recognizable people in the country. He was just a normal person. For years, he even listed his number in the phone book.

Walter was a favorite of everyone: My wife and sister both adored him. So did all of the waitstaff, the majority of whom were too young to even know who he was. He was the one celebrity other celebrities would ask to meet, which was a little difficult, because everyone knew we did not allow our celebrity customers to be approached—by anyone. It didn't matter if it was an eight-year-old kid meekly asking the hostess if it was okay to ask for Mr. Cronkite's autograph or Meg Ryan. I didn't want it happening in my restaurant.

Walter was the only person I would save a parking place for. Parking at the Home Port was always a problem—too many cars and not enough land. If you've been there, you know. People would get very creative with their parking. There was nothing like looking out and seeing a Range Rover wedged between two Mercedes so tightly, the driver had to crawl out the sunroof. The last couple of years of Betsy's life, it was hard for her to get from the parking lot to the restaurant. They still came regularly, though. It couldn't have been easy for her. One night Betsy came in alone. My sister asked if Walter was coming. "We've been driving around for an hour trying to find a parking place," Betsy said. My sister came back and told me about their problem. "That won't do," I said. Everyone agreed.

After Walter and Betsy's meal, I went out to see how everything was. As always, they were incredibly nice. "I hear you had some trouble parking," I said after a rather lengthy conversation. Walter chuckled and shook his head the way he did. "The next time you come in, call me in the afternoon and I'll make sure you have a place to park," I told him. Now, Walter was never one to use his celebrity for anything other than a good cause, but for this he seemed truly grateful. Sure enough, the next week I got a call. "Hi, Will. I'm going to take you up on that offer for a parking place," he said. I went out and marked off a place right by the door.

That will always be his parking place. That's the way it is.

The Home Port postcard, circa 1980

Shrimp Bisque

1. Melt butter in a large heavy-bottomed pan. Sauté onion, celery, and carrots over medium heat for 5–6 minutes.
2. Add garlic, shrimp shells, and 1 pound of shrimp. Cook for 5 minutes.
3. Remove pan from heat and flambé with brandy. (Please be careful.) Add tomatoes, water, vegetable juice, bay leaves, and bread crumbs. Simmer for 15–20 minutes or until thickened, stirring occasionally.
4. Remove from heat and allow to cool for 15–20 minutes.
5. Puree in a blender or food processor until smooth. Strain through a fine mesh strainer.
6. Add heavy cream and remaining 1 pound of shrimp, shrimp or lobster base, sherry, Tabasco, and Worcestershire sauce. Add salt and pepper to taste.
7. Reheat over medium heat for 5 minutes or until shrimp is cooked.
8. Serve in warm bowls, garnished with parsley.

SERVES 8–10

4 tablespoons butter

½ cup chopped onion

½ cup chopped celery

1 carrot, peeled and chopped

2 garlic cloves, chopped

2 pounds shrimp (36–40 count), peeled and deveined (save shells)

¼ cup brandy

2 medium tomatoes, chopped

1 quart water

1 cup vegetable juice, such as V-8

4 bay leaves

1 cup fresh bread crumbs

1 cup heavy cream

2 tablespoons shrimp or lobster base

¼ cup dry sherry

4–5 drops Tabasco

½ teaspoon Worcestershire sauce

Salt and white pepper to taste

Chopped fresh flat-leaf parsley for garnish

Mussel Soup

3 tablespoons extra-virgin olive oil

½ cup finely chopped shallots

4 garlic cloves, minced

½ teaspoon dried thyme

½ teaspoon dried basil

4 bay leaves

Zest of 1 lemon

1½ cups white wine

4 cups clam juice

½ teaspoon Old Bay or preferred seafood spice

6 pounds mussels, rinsed, scrubbed, and debearded

Juice of 1 lemon

Salt and pepper to taste

Chopped fresh flat-leaf parsley for garnish

1. In a large pot with a tight-fitting lid, heat olive oil, shallots, garlic, thyme, basil, bay leaves, and lemon zest for 3 minutes over medium heat.
2. Add wine, clam juice, and Old Bay and bring to a boil.
3. Once boiling, add mussels. Shaking pot occasionally, cook until mussels open, about 5–8 minutes depending on their size. Discard any mussels that did not open.
4. Add lemon juice, a pinch of salt, and a generous amount of fresh ground pepper.
5. Give mussels a quick stir and serve in a large bowl with the broth, garnished with parsley. Pair with a crusty bread.

SERVES 8–10

Lobster Stew

1. Melt butter in a large sauté pan. Add lobster meat and cook over medium-low heat for 1 minute.
2. In a separate pot, heat the remaining ingredients except salt and pepper over medium heat until warm.
3. Add the lobster meat and butter to the pot and heat until very hot. Do not bring to a boil.
4. Add salt and pepper to taste and serve in warm bowls.

SERVES 6–8

4 tablespoons butter

1 pound lobster meat, chopped

1 small garlic clove, minced

1 teaspoon paprika

2 bay leaves

1 tablespoon lobster base

½ cup vegetable juice, such as V-8

5 cups light cream

¼ cup dry sherry

Salt and pepper to taste

Oyster Stew

1 pint oysters, shucked

2 cups heavy cream

3–4 drops Tabasco

5–6 drops Worcestershire sauce

3 tablespoons butter

Salt and pepper to taste

Paprika

1. Drain oysters, saving liquid (oyster liquor).
2. In a large pot, heat cream, oyster liquor, Tabasco, and Worcestershire sauce over medium heat for 5 minutes. Do not let boil.
3. In a separate pan, melt butter and sauté oysters for 2 minutes over medium heat.
4. Add contents of sauté pan to pot and continue heating over medium heat for 3 minutes. Do not let boil.
5. Add salt and pepper to taste.
6. Serve in warm bowls. Sprinkle with paprika and serve with oyster crackers.

SERVES 4–6

Seafood Stew

I added this dish to the Home Port menu in the mid-'90s because I wanted to offer an alternative to our cream-based quahog chowder. It is a combination of French, Spanish, and Italian flavors. Don't let the number of ingredients scare you—this recipe is really quite simple.

1. Place all the ingredients except the seafood in a large heavy-bottomed pot. Bring to a boil.
2. Reduce heat and simmer for 15 minutes, stirring occasionally.
3. Add all the seafood except the lobster meat. Increase heat until a light boil begins.
4. Reduce heat and simmer for 10 minutes, stirring occasionally.
5. Add lobster meat just before serving. Salt and pepper to taste.

SERVES 10–12

Options: Try adding white wine. For a little spicier stew, try using a hotter salsa, red pepper flakes, or Tabasco.

1 teaspoon saffron

1 medium-large onion, cut into ¼-inch-thick slices

1 medium green pepper, cut into ¼-inch-thick slices

1 medium yellow pepper, cut into ¼-inch-thick slices

1 garlic clove, thinly sliced

3 bay leaves

¼ cup chopped fresh parsley

1 tablespoon Italian spices

1 cup marinara sauce

2 cups diced tomatoes

1½ teaspoons Worcestershire sauce

1 cup salsa

1 cup vegetable juice, such as V-8

4 cups fish stock or clam juice

½ pound sea scallops, halved

½ pound shrimp (12–15 count), peeled and deveined

18 mussels, rinsed, scrubbed, and debearded

18 littleneck clams, rinsed and scrubbed

2 pounds firm fish (halibut, bass, or swordfish), cut into bite-size pieces

½ pound fresh lobster meat

Salt and pepper to taste

Clams and Mussels

The quahog is the hard-shell variety of the wide-ranging clam family and is more robust in flavor—a trademark of most traditional Martha's Vineyard chowder recipes, including the Home Port's. Most traditional mainland clam chowders utilize the larger, sweeter, less flavorful sea clam variety of clam.

The name quahog is derived from the Wampanoag Indian word p'quaghaug. When opened, portions of the inside of the shell are a pearly violet color. The indigenous people used this part of the shell, called wampum, as currency.

Quahogs can be found on the sandy bottoms of saltwater lagoons and ponds from Canada to Florida. In fish markets, they are generally found in three grades: littlenecks, which are 2 inches across and best enjoyed raw on the half shell; cherrystones, which range from 2 to 3 inches across and are generally steamed; and chowder-grade quahogs, which span more than 3 inches across.

Mussels were, for a long time, one of the most underutilized seafoods around. On Martha's Vineyard, I could literally walk out the back door of the restaurant and collect all the mussels I could ever need. Only recently have mussels become more popular. Today mussels can be found in most fish markets and many supermarkets.

As with all seafood, make sure your mussels are fresh: When did they come in, and when were they harvested? With mussels, the question to ask is whether they are wild or cultivated. Wild mussels can sometimes have tiny crabs in them. The crabs are harmless, and even enhance the flavor a little, but provide an unexpected crunch. For that reason, I prefer cultivated mussels, usually 2 to 3 inches across. Mussels have a hairlike covering called a beard, which holds them together in clusters in the water. Whenever possible, buy mussels that still have that beard, and then use a knife to debeard them just before cooking. Before they are cooked, mussels should open and close fairly freely. Discard any that do not open and close completely.

Littlenecks on the Half Shell

The littleneck is the most tender of the quahog variety and best for eating raw. For the novice, littlenecks can be a little challenging to open. Some people slice between the shells on the round side. This technique is fine for larger quahogs that will be chopped up later, but for littlenecks on the half shell, open them at the point of the hinge. As I like to say, "It's why God gave them a hinge in the first place." They will pop right open and leave the meat inside undamaged. Purists will eat their littlenecks without any lemon or cocktail sauce so they get that full, briny taste. But any way you eat them, you know they're going to be good.

Shucking Clams and Quahogs

Step 1: *Tightly hold a clam knife blade two inches from its tip.*

Step 2: *Insert the tip at the clam's hinge and gently rock until the top shell releases.*

Step 3: *Slide your knife blade against the top shell to sever the connecting muscle. Discard the shell.*

Step 4: *Slide your knife blade under the clam to separate it from the bottom shell.*

Shucking Oysters

Step 1: Working on a stable surface, place a towel under the oyster, with the side of the oyster facing up.

Step 2: Insert your knife at the oyster's hinge to pry the top shell loose.

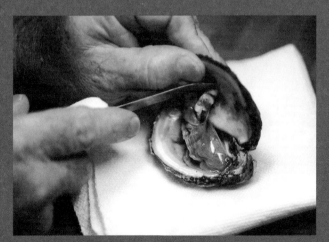

Step 3: Slide your knife blade against the top shell to sever the connecting muscle. Discard the shell.

Step 4: Slide your knife under the oyster to separate it from the bottom shell.

Stuffed Quahogs

8 tablespoons butter

1 cup chopped onion, cut into ¼-inch pieces

1 cup chopped celery, cut into ¼-inch pieces

½ cup chopped green pepper, cut into ¼-inch pieces

3 garlic cloves, minced

24 large quahogs, steamed open, meat chopped into ¼-inch pieces (save shells)

2 pints sea clams, minced

2 tablespoons chopped fresh parsley

⅛ teaspoon poultry seasoning

1 teaspoon dried dill

¼ teaspoon freshly ground black pepper

1 teaspoon paprika

4–5 drops Tabasco

5–6 drops Worcestershire sauce

1 pound panko bread crumbs

People are always asking what the secret to the Home Port's stuffed quahogs is. It's simple, really: lots and lots of extra clam meat. In my opinion, most stuffed quahog recipes—or "stuffies," as they are called in other places—have too much bread crumbs and spices and not enough meat. At the Home Port, we featured the taste of the clam, not everything else.

1. Preheat oven to 400°F.
2. Melt butter in a large nonstick frying pan over medium heat. Add onions, celery, and green peppers and sauté for 3 minutes.
3. Add garlic and continue sautéing for 2 minutes, stirring frequently.
4. Add all the other ingredients except bread crumbs and cook for 3 minutes.
5. Remove from heat and allow to cool (approximately 10 minutes).
6. Mix in bread crumbs. The stuffing should be very moist. If not, add a little clam broth or butter. If the stuffing is soggy, add a small amount of bread crumbs until mixture is moist.
7. Fill quahog shells with stuffing and place on a baking sheet.
8. Bake until stuffing is browned, about 20–25 minutes. A little crunch on top is desirable.
9. Serve with red cocktail sauce (page 185) and lemon wedges.

SERVES 4–6

Clams Casino

The combination of spices, herbs, bacon, and bread crumbs with the flavor of fresh clams makes this a fantastic appetizer.

1. Preheat oven to 400°F.
2. Scrub clams with a stiff-bristled brush. Open clams, loosening the meat from the shell. Keep in bottom shell and arrange on a baking sheet.
3. Spread at least 1 teaspoon of casino butter on each clam. Sprinkle each clam with bread crumbs.
4. Bake for 10 minutes or until bread crumbs are lightly toasted.
5. Serve with lemon wedges.

SERVES 4–6

24 littleneck or cherrystone clams

½ cup casino butter (page 201)

1 cup panko bread crumbs

Clam Fritters

1½ quarts canola oil

1 pint shucked sea clams, drained (save liquid) and minced

½ cup evaporated milk

1 cup pancake mix

2 tablespoons cornmeal

1 tablespoon clam base

¼ teaspoon white pepper

½ teaspoon Old Bay or preferred seafood spice

½ teaspoon dried dill

Not many places still serve up these tasty little treats, as the trend toward slightly more healthy appetizers continues to grip the dining public. But do yourself a favor and try these at least once. You can always go for a nice long walk afterwards.

1. Heat 3 inches of oil in a 10- to 12-inch heavy-bottomed pot to 360°F.
2. In a mixing bowl, combine all the ingredients, stirring gently.
3. When oil reaches 360°F, spoon in the batter 1 tablespoon at a time. Use two spoons to keep your fingers away from the hot oil. Be careful not to crowd the pot.
4. Roll fritters in oil once they have browned lightly so they cook evenly on all sides.
5. When golden brown, remove fritters and let cool slightly on a paper towel to remove excess oil.
6. Serve with tartar sauce (page 186), cocktail sauce (pages 185 and 186), or dill sauce (page 190) and lemon wedges.

SERVES 4–6

Options: Add chopped spinach, cilantro, or parsley to the batter for added flavor.

Steamed Clams

Often called steamers or soft-shell clams, these beauties are the same clams used for frying. There is no shucking involved, just an overnight soaking in seawater to remove the sand. If seawater is not an option, cold tap water and a small handful of salt and cornmeal (the cornmeal, for some reason, causes the little buggers to spit out any sand they have ingested). When not using seawater, only soak for a couple of hours before steaming.

Purists prefer their clams cooked and served with the broth and melted butter for dipping. Others will cook them with white wine, dry vermouth, and a variety of herbs and spices. No matter how you cook them, don't forget the broth, lemon wedges, and plenty of hot melted butter.

½–¾ cup water per pound of clams

1–2 pounds steamer clams per person, rinsed well

2 bay leaves

2 garlic cloves, coarsely chopped

Melted butter for dipping

Lemon wedges

1. Bring water to a boil, drop in all the ingredients, and cover.
2. Bring water back to a boil and cook for 5–6 minutes or until clams have opened.
3. Remove clams to a serving bowl, and strain broth through a coffee filter.
4. Serve clams with broth, melted butter, and lemon wedges.

Options: Add fresh basil, thyme, and 1 cup of white wine to liven up the flavor of the broth.

Steamed Mussels

1 pound mussels per person
½ cup water per pound of mussels
Melted butter for dipping
Lemon wedges

1. Rinse, scrub, and debeard mussels.
2. Place mussels and water in a pot and cover. Bring to a boil.
3. Continue boiling for 3–4 minutes or until mussels open.
4. Remove mussels to a serving bowl, and strain broth through a coffee filter.
5. Serve mussels with broth, melted butter, and lemon wedges.

Options: Use ¼ cup water and ¼ cup white wine per pound of mussels. Herbs like chopped shallots, garlic, basil, and thyme all enhance the flavor of mussels.

OYSTERS

I have often wondered, and I'm sure I'm not alone in this, who was the first person to crack an oyster and slurp it down—and how hungry must he have been? I must say I'm damn glad he did, though.

There are more than 200 varieties of these somewhat fragile bivalve mollusks. Over the years disease and the continual loss of natural habitat have devastated oyster populations throughout North America. But thanks to conservation efforts, oysters are making a comeback. In North America, they are found in ponds and saltwater creeks from Canada to the Gulf of Mexico.

It is generally true that oysters (and other shellfish) should not be consumed—raw, anyway—in months without an *r* in them. But contrary to popular belief, this is not because they are inedible. It is during the warm months of May through August that the oysters grow and the colonies revitalize. In many places, it is illegal to harvest oysters during these months. They are still available, but they are not going to be as tasty as oysters harvested in *r* months.

I have to admit, oysters on the half shell are one of my greatest indulgences. My love affair with oysters started back when I was in engineering school in Boston. I spent more than a few hours in the Union Oyster Bar slurping down these wonderful little jewels with a cold beer or two. And no, in all my experience, I have found no reason to believe that they are an aphrodisiac. Having eaten twelve dozen one Sunday afternoon thirty years ago at Pete's Oyster Bar in Panama City, Florida, I was no more amorous toward anyone—or anyone toward me—than I was when I sat down.

I Know That Voice

At the Home Port, I liked to take a break in the afternoon. Not long, thirty minutes or an hour, just to get out of the kitchen for a while before all of the craziness of dinner got going. Usually I would go for a little walk down to the docks, and sometimes I'd stop in at Larson's Fish Market to say hello to everyone. Larson's was the daytime hub in Menemsha, much the same way the Home Port was in the evening. They had a wonderful raw bar there. It was always busy, with people coming in off the beach for lunch. Sometimes I liked to go back and shuck oysters and clams for people—sort of a busman's holiday. There was something relaxing about being back there and prying open those wonderful, delicious little creatures and talking to people.

One afternoon I went down and hopped behind the counter of the raw bar, like I always did, and picked up a knife and started shucking away. Trish Larson, a near and dear friend for as long as I have been on the Island (as has the entire Larson family), was back there hard at work. She was an incredible shucker. The speed and precision with which she shucked made me look like I was doing it for the first time—and I can shuck faster than most people I know. But with Trish, it was like she had four arms. Just as I went to pop open that first oyster, she stopped what she was doing and pointed her knife at me like she was going to shuck me open next. "Put down that knife," she said. "Step away from the oysters." I could see she wasn't joking. "Did I do something?" I asked. I was really worried I had done something to make her angry. She laughed a little, to put me at ease. "These are for Paul Newman," she said. "No one shucks his oysters but me."

Now, I knew he was on the Island. He had been coming here for a number of years and had been in the Home Port a few times for dinner. "You sure that's all you want to do for him?" I asked her. She pointed her knife at me again. "Get out," she said. I made my exit and walked to the end of the dock, down along the beach, and back to the restaurant.

One of the more glamorous parts of owning a restaurant is that when something needs to be done that no one wants to do—like scrubbing out the trash cans—you are the one who ultimately winds up doing it. When the weather gets hot, the trash cans develop a certain funk when they are not scrubbed out often. When I came back from my walk, I could smell that the trash cans were getting ripe, and, not finding anyone to delegate the chore to, I started on it myself.

I was scrubbing away when I heard someone behind me say, "Who do I pay for the ice?" Even halfway inside a trash can, that voice was unmistakable. I crawled out of the can and turned around and sure enough, Paul Newman was standing there looking at me with those incredible blue eyes. I'm not afraid to say it: He was a damn handsome man. Looking at him, face-to-face, I understood why Trish didn't want me around when he came in. "Mr. Newman," I said. "The ice is on me. It's a pleasure to meet you." He put out his hand. I did the best to wipe the trash can slime off mine and we shook hands. "You don't have to do that," he said. "I don't want you getting in trouble with your boss." I couldn't help but laugh. "He won't mind," I said. He thanked me and got into his old station wagon and drove away.

A couple of days later, I was outside putting a delivery in the walk-in coolers. Darren Wright was helping me. Darren was a local kid who worked for me for a few years. He was an incredibly talented young man who went on to be Todd English's right-hand man in Boston. I was lucky to have him for as long as I did. We were out going through everything and getting it put away when an old station wagon came screeching to a stop in the parking lot, kicking up a giant cloud of dust. This was before the parking lot was paved. When it didn't rain for a couple of days, it would get incredibly dusty. Darren, never one to mince words, yelled at the driver of the wagon even before he got out of the car, "Who do you think you are? Steve McQueen?" The driver got out and said, "No, but I know him." Darren then realized who he was. Our visitor went to the ice cooler and came over to pay me. "Don't worry about it," I said. He gave us a wink, got in his car, and pulled out of the parking lot, gunning it, spinning the tires of the old station wagon, kicking up a bunch of gravel and dust. "Steve McQueen?" I said. Darren just shrugged. From up on the hill, Mr. Newman honked and gave us a wave.

Oysters on the Half Shell

There is always something exciting about buying fresh oysters at a fish market. The sound those hard shells make clanking together always makes me hungry. When buying oysters, figure that most people will eat six each when served as an appetizer. If the night centers around these delectable little morsels, figure close to a dozen per person. There will always be people who won't touch them (they don't know what they are missing) and those who will eat one after another.

As soon as you get home, wash the oysters in cold water using a hard-bristled scrub brush and savor the wonderful fresh smell. Make sure the water is ice cold. Once the oysters are clean, place them in a colander and cover them with ice. Be sure to put a bowl under the colander to collect the melting ice. Cover it all with a damp towel (paper will work if you don't want to designate a cloth towel for this purpose) and place in the refrigerator until you are ready to devour these beauties.

For those who have never shucked before, it can be somewhat intimidating. But after the first two or three, you'll find it's easy. The best tool you can get for this is an oyster knife, which can be found at any fish market. You'll also need two kitchen towels.

Fold one towel in quarters and lay it on the counter. Unless you're a pro, you're going to want to use the counter to keep things steady. Place the oyster round-side down on the towel and use the second towel to hold down the oyster. You will want to do this because there are all kinds of sharp little edges on the shells—one slip and you have a nasty little gash in your hand. Insert the knife between the shells at the pointed corner of the oyster. There should be a small indentation there. Move the knife in a rocking motion

until the shells open slightly. Once you have a little room to work, gingerly move the knife blade in across the top of the shell toward the back. Avoid hitting any of the meat with the knife. Once this is done, the top shell should pop right off. Now carefully slide the knife blade under the exposed oyster meat and separate the connector muscle from the bottom shell. The meat will pop up a little and settle back into its place.

Place each shucked shell on a platter that has been covered with crushed ice, and serve with lemon wedges and your wonderful homemade cocktail sauce (pages 185 and 186). For a little different flavor, try a mignonette sauce (page 187). Now comes the best part. Enjoy!

Stuffed Oysters

24 oysters, scrubbed and
  shucked
2 cups herb stuffing (page 203)
2 tablespoons butter
¼ cup grated Parmesan cheese

1. Preheat oven to 400°F.
2. Place shucked oysters on a baking sheet. Cover each oyster with stuffing.
3. Melt butter and drizzle an equal amount over each oyster. Sprinkle with cheese.
4. Bake for 12–14 minutes or until stuffing turns golden brown.

SERVES 4–6

Oysters Casino

It's like going to Las Vegas: There's a casino for just about everyone.

1. Preheat oven to 400°F.
2. Shuck oysters, loosening the meat from the shell. Keep in the bottom shell and arrange on a baking sheet.
3. Spread at least 1 teaspoon of casino butter on each oyster. Sprinkle each oyster with bread crumbs.
4. Bake for 10 minutes or until bread crumbs are lightly toasted.
5. Serve with lemon wedges.

SERVES 4–6

24 oysters, scrubbed
½ cup casino butter (page 201)
1 cup panko bread crumbs

Oysters with Ginger Saffron Sauce

24 oysters, scrubbed, shucked, meat removed, and strained (save liquid and bottom shell)

1 cup ginger saffron sauce (page 191)

Fresh ground black pepper to taste

Chopped fresh flat-leaf parsley for garnish

1. Preheat oven to 450°F.
2. Return strained oysters to bottom shells and place on a baking sheet.
3. Top each oyster with ginger saffron sauce. Grind fresh black pepper over each oyster to taste.
4. On middle oven rack, bake for 8–10 minutes or until sauce begins to brown.
5. Garnish with chopped parsley.

SERVES 4–6

Options: Chives or cilantro can be substituted for garnish.

Oysters Rockefeller

It's all but impossible to go to a seafood restaurant and not see a version of this dish. It's a tried-and-true favorite. Here's my version. I may be biased, but I haven't found better yet.

1. Preheat oven to 450°F.
2. Melt butter in a large nonstick frying pan. Add shallots and celery and cook over medium heat for 3 minutes.
3. Add spinach, garlic, tarragon, parsley, Tabasco, and Worcestershire sauce. Cover and cook for 3 minutes or until spinach has wilted. Remove from heat.
4. Put contents of pan along with bread crumbs and Pernod in a food processor and pulse until mixture is minced.
5. Place oyster shells on a baking sheet and put an oyster in each shell.
6. Top each oyster with spinach mixture and sprinkle with Parmesan cheese.
7. Bake for 8–10 minutes or until cheese is golden brown.

SERVES 4–6

6 tablespoons butter

¼ cup chopped shallots

¼ cup chopped celery

1 pound fresh spinach, rinsed and stems removed

2 garlic cloves, chopped

1 tablespoon chopped fresh tarragon

½ cup chopped fresh parsley

3–4 drops Tabasco

3–4 drops Worcestershire sauce

½ cup panko bread crumbs

1 tablespoon Pernod or anisette

36 oysters, scrubbed, shucked, and meat removed (save bottom shells)

½ cup grated Parmesan cheese

Oyster Fritters

1½ quarts canola oil

1 pint shucked oysters, halved
   or quartered and strained

½ cup evaporated milk

1 cup pancake mix

2 tablespoons cornmeal

¼ tablespoon white pepper

½ teaspoon Old Bay or
   preferred seafood spice

½ teaspoon dried dill

Another great fritter (is there such a thing as a bad fritter?) option. To take a little of the labor out of preparation, kindly ask your local fish market to shuck the oysters for you.

1. Heat 3 inches of oil in a 10- to 12-inch heavy-bottomed pot to 360°F.
2. Mix all ingredients together in a bowl, stirring gently.
3. When oil reaches 360°F, spoon in the batter 1 tablespoon at a time. Use two spoons to keep your fingers away from the hot oil. Be careful not to crowd the pot.
4. Roll fritters in oil once they have browned lightly so they cook evenly on all sides.
5. When golden brown, remove fritters and let cool slightly on a paper towel to remove excess oil.
6. Serve with tartar sauce (page 186), cocktail sauce (pages 185 and 186), or dill sauce (page 190) and lemon wedges.

SERVES 4–6

Options: Add chopped spinach, cilantro, or parsley to the batter for added flavor.

LOBSTER

Lobster Cocktail

If it's in the budget, there is no better way to start a meal than with a little lobster cocktail. It is delicious and makes an impressive presentation.

2 1- to 1¼-pound lobsters
Red cocktail sauce (page 185)

1. Boil lobsters (see page 89) and chill for at least 2 hours in the refrigerator.
2. Once chilled, split lobsters in half and remove stomach and intestinal tract.
3. Crack open lobsters and remove top half of claw shell.
4. Refill the stomach cavity with red cocktail sauce.
5. Place on a chilled plate with salad greens and lemon wedges.

SERVES 4–6

Lobster Cakes

5 tablespoons butter

2 tablespoons minced shallots

1 tablespoon minced green pepper

1 teaspoon minced garlic

1 cup panko bread crumbs

¼ cup finely chopped fresh parsley

1 teaspoon Old Bay or preferred seafood spice

1 egg, lightly beaten

¼ cup mayonnaise

Salt and pepper to taste

1 pound lobster meat, roughly chopped

4 tablespoons vegetable oil

Lobster lovers will love this alternative to the more traditional crab cakes. Keep in mind you will need two hours for the lobster cakes to set in the refrigerator before cooking. You'll find the cakes hold together better while cooking if they are chilled. I like to serve mine on a bed of fresh watercress or other leafy greens. On the side, try aioli (page 190), red cocktail sauce (page 185), or tartar sauce (page 186).

1. Melt 1 tablespoon butter in a nonstick frying pan. Sauté shallots, green pepper, and garlic over medium heat for 3 minutes, stirring frequently. Be sure not to burn the garlic.

2. Transfer sautéed vegetables to a large mixing bowl. Add ¼ cup bread crumbs, parsley, Old Bay, egg, mayonnaise, a pinch of salt, and a pinch of pepper and mix.

3. Add lobster meat and mix thoroughly.

4. Form 8 equal-size patties (should be about ⅓ cup each). Sprinkle extra bread crumbs on both sides of patties.

5. Place patties on a tray and refrigerate for a minimum of 2 hours.

6. Melt 2 tablespoons butter and 2 tablespoons oil in a nonstick frying pan over medium-high heat. When oil is hot, sauté 4 cakes for 2–3 minutes on each side or until golden brown. Remove cakes from pan. Add remaining butter and oil and sauté 4 remaining cakes.

7. Serve immediately or keep warm in the oven.

MAKES 8 LOBSTER CAKES

Lobster-Stuffed Deviled Eggs

This twist on an old party favorite will ensure those party invitations keep coming.

1. Remove yolks from eggs and combine yolks with remaining ingredients in a large mixing bowl.
2. Fill the yolk cavities with mixture.
3. Chill for 1 hour before serving.

SERVES 4–6

8 hardboiled eggs, peeled and halved

¼ pound lobster meat, chopped into ¼- to ½-inch pieces

¼ cup mayonnaise

1 tablespoon minced shallots

1 tablespoon minced celery

½ teaspoon Old Bay or preferred seafood spice

SHRIMP

Shrimp Cocktail

1 quart court bouillon (page 184) per pound of shrimp

1½ teaspoons Old Bay or preferred seafood spice per pound of shrimp

Juice of 1 lemon per pound of shrimp

16–20-count shrimp, peeled and deveined with tail on

Unless you live in the coastal Southeast, most of the shrimp you will find at the fish markets are previously frozen. Yes, there is a difference between fresh shrimp and the frozen stuff. If you can't get fresh, make sure that the frozen shrimp has not already been cooked. Unlike many things, in this case, size doesn't matter. At the Home Port, I used 16–20 count per pound. It comes down to personal taste and what is available.

Take a few extra minutes to cook the shrimp yourself. I boil my shrimp in court bouillon. That's the great thing about court bouillon: You can keep it in the freezer and use it over and over, and it just gets better with each use. If you don't happen to have any court bouillon on hand, use water with a good dash of salt, lemon juice, and bay leaves.

1. Bring court bouillon, Old Bay, and lemon juice to a boil. (Toss in the spent lemon for the extra flavor the boiling process will extract from it.) Add shrimp and stir.
2. Remove shrimp as soon as they begin to turn pink (this should be about the same time the water begins to boil again) and place in a large bowl of ice water as quickly as possible.
3. Drain off water and place shrimp in the refrigerator for 1 hour before serving.
4. Serve on shredded lettuce with lemon wedges and red cocktail sauce (page 185).

Options: Instead of red cocktail sauce, try dill sauce (page 190) or green cocktail sauce (page 186).

Shrimp Scampi

Though usually thought of as a main course served over rice or pasta, shrimp scampi makes a great starter served without a starch.

1. Melt butter in a large nonstick frying pan over low heat. Add garlic and cook for 3 minutes, stirring frequently. Be careful not to burn the garlic.
2. Add shrimp, Italian spices, lemon juice, and sherry. Turn up heat to medium and cook until the shrimp are pink on both sides.
3. Remove from heat. Add basil and parsley and stir.
4. Serve on a warm plate with slices of lightly toasted crusty bread.

SERVES 4–6

Option: Use scallops instead of shrimp.

4 tablespoons butter

1½ teaspoons minced garlic

1 pound shrimp (16–20 count), peeled and deveined

½ teaspoon Italian spices

1½ teaspoons lemon juice

¾ teaspoon dry sherry

2 tablespoons chopped fresh basil

1 tablespoon chopped fresh parsley

Ham-Wrapped Shrimp

1 pound shrimp (16–20 count), peeled and deveined

½ pound thinly sliced ham of choice

Extra-virgin olive oil

I usually use Italian ham with this dish, though bacon (blanched) is a very good alternative. I prefer ham because it has a milder flavor than bacon and does not overpower the taste of the shrimp. Thinly sliced proscuitto, capicola, or serrano ham all work wonderfully for this purpose.

1. Preheat oven to 325°F.
2. Rinse and pat dry shrimp.
3. Wrap each shrimp with ham and rub with olive oil. Place on a baking sheet.
4. Bake for 10–12 minutes or until shrimp is a delicate pink color.
5. Serve on a warm plate with salsa and corn chips.

SERVES 4–6

Option: Use scallops in place of shrimp.

Shrimp Jalapeño

This recipe is on the spicy side. With a mild-tasting seafood like shrimp, the flavor can sometimes get lost when preparing it with various spices, which is okay with dishes like this. Just be careful not to overcook the shrimp. The texture of the shrimp is the true star of this delicious appetizer.

1. Heat olive oil in a large nonstick frying pan over medium-low heat. Add jalapeños, garlic, and shallots. Sauté for 2–3 minutes, stirring frequently so garlic does not burn.
2. Add shrimp. Cook until pink on one side.
3. Flip shrimp and add tomato. Cook until shrimp is pink on both sides.
4. Season with Tabasco and salt and pepper to taste.
5. Serve on a warm serving plate, sprinkled with parsley, with lightly toasted slices of crusty bread.

SERVES 4–6

3 tablespoons extra-virgin olive oil

2 medium jalapeños, chopped into ¼-inch pieces (remove seeds and membrane for milder flavor)

2 garlic cloves, minced

1 tablespoon minced shallots

1 pound shrimp (16–20 count), peeled and deveined

1 medium tomato, seeds removed, chopped into ½-inch pieces

Tabasco to taste

Salt and pepper to taste

Coarsely chopped flat-leaf parsley for garnish

A Flower by Any Other Name

I remember the first time I heard Beverly Sills was coming for dinner. It was back when I was working for Chet Cummens. Everyone was excited. "Who's Beverly Sills?" I asked. "Duhh," someone said. "She's only the most famous opera singer in the world." I have to admit, I had never heard of her. I spent the rest of the afternoon trying to picture what the most famous opera singer in the world would look like. Let's just say I was wrong on all accounts. Beverly Sills was beautiful. She had this flowing strawberry blond hair and a peachy complexion. She was one of the most elegant women to ever grace the Home Port—and there have been a lot of elegant women in over the years. The first time I heard a recording of her sing, I was absolutely floored. I had no idea what she was saying, but it didn't matter. It was, and still is, one of the most beautiful things I have ever heard.

Over the years, Ms. Sills became one of my favorite customers. She would come in four or five times a season, and had a standing reservation on July 12, her birthday. I always get a little emotional thinking about her. I can't say enough about how wonderful she was to everyone, kind and sweet. In a television interview a few years before her death, she even went as far as saying the Home Port was her favorite restaurant on the Vineyard.

It was always a Home Port tradition for the staff to sing "Happy Birthday" to customers celebrating at the Home Port. Ms. Sills wouldn't let us sing for her. She didn't want the attention. That's the kind of person she was. A few years back, I went out to wish her a happy birthday. For fun I asked her in what key she would like the staff to sing "Happy Birthday" to her. She grabbed my wrist with her tiny hand, looked at me very seriously, and said, "They better not." But she could only keep a straight face for a second.

A couple years before Ms. Sills passed away, my wife, Madeline, and I were out shopping for flowers to plant around the outside of the restaurant. Finding flowering plants hearty enough to survive out there was tricky with all of the saltwater around. About the only flower that really thrived was iris. We were going through all of the different varieties of iris when I found one with wonderful pink blossoms. I showed Madeline. "Look what they are called," she said, holding up the tag. Beverly Sills Iris it said. The blossoms looked like her: delicate and bright and pretty. Of course, I bought them and planted them down by the pond, and for several years they bloomed every spring, bright and beautiful.

Ms. Sills passed away in June 2007. The next spring the iris, her iris, did not bloom.

SCALLOPS

Salt of the Sea

You'd be hard-pressed to find better scallops than what is pulled out of the waters around Martha's Vineyard. Scallop season begins in November and, when the crop is good, can run through the winter. The scallops are shucked right there on the dock and taken to local fish markets for processing. Scallops are terribly fragile creatures—something as simple as a rainstorm during spawning season can all but ruin a year's catch.

Chet Cummens loved to scallop. Every year he would personally catch all of the Home Port's scallops for the upcoming season. When I took over, I wanted to keep with tradition, so I took it up. And I have to be honest: I really had no clue where to even begin scalloping. Thankfully, I had some help. In fact, I couldn't have learned from anyone better.

Hershel West was a true local character—a Cricker, as Menemsha natives are called. They called him the Mayor of Menemsha because he knew everyone and everything. He was gruff and unkempt, but generally a happy man. He lived on his boat in the harbor with a scruffy black toy poodle that followed him everywhere. He was the kind of guy who either liked you or didn't, but at least you always knew right where you stood. We were buddies. He took me under his wing. Hershel was a true fisherman in every sense of the word.

He could accurately predict the weather just by looking at the sky on a perfectly clear day, and tell you exactly where you could find whatever it was you wanted to catch. And he could shuck a scallop faster than anyone I have ever seen. In his younger days, Hershel was pretty wild. Chet would tell me stories. Hershel liked to have a good time. By the time I knew him, he had mellowed—and dried—out considerably. Age does that to you, I guess.

Hershel was a local celebrity of sorts, long before a casting director tapped him to be Robert Shaw's sidekick in *Jaws*. That was a very exciting time in Menemsha. *Jaws* was the first of a long list of movies filmed there, and it put Menemsha on the map. Just about everyone there was an extra in the movie. Unfortunately, I missed all of the excitement—I was in Boston working at Pier 4. When they were casting extras, the casting director needed someone who looked the part of an authentic fisherman. You don't get much more authentic than Hershel. He says he didn't even want to be in the movie, that they just saw him and it took quite a bit of convincing to talk him into it. (I don't necessarily believe him, though.) They hired him on the spot. The next day when he showed up at the appointed time, he was hardly recognizable: clean-shaven and dressed in his best clothes. He looked presentable. Let's just say Steven Spielberg was not happy with the new and improved Hershel. "Go back and put on those old smelly clothes and come back looking like yourself," he told him. Hershel did, and spent the next few weeks in the background. He was one of the only locals with a speaking part in the movie. For a long time there was a giant poster of him at Universal Studios. People still come to Menemsha looking for him, wanting his autograph.

Despite my expert tutelage, I can't say I particularly enjoyed the scalloping itself. Spending time on the water with Hershel was what I really liked. Scalloping was hard, cold, miserable work. You go out in a small boat because the scallops are in the shallow water, so you're exposed to the weather. There is a reason people only come to the Vineyard in the summer. December is miserably cold and wet. When I decided I was going to scallop, I went out and bought everything I would need. I had a little 19-foot skiff and all the gear. Hershel showed me how to fish the drags along the bottom. It was tricky because scallops swim. You could see them trying to outswim the drags. On good days it was really satisfying, but there were plenty of bad days, too, pulling up nothing but old shoes and beer bottles.

I hate to say it, but what I liked best about scalloping was eating them fresh out of the water. There is nothing better than a fresh, raw scallop. Every time we brought in the drag, I would find some nice, big, juicy-looking ones and pop them open, clean out the guts, and dip them overboard to get them good and clean and salty. They would just melt in your mouth. Hershel would get mad at me because some days I would eat nearly everything I caught.

Smoked scallops (page 70)

Broiled Scallops

Always a crowd pleaser and easy to prepare!

1. Preheat broiler.
2. Place scallops on broiler pan. Brush liberally with melted butter. Sprinkle with paprika.
3. Place pan on top rack (3–4 inches from heat source) and cook for 3–4 minutes. Bay scallops or smaller sea scallops will need only 2–3 minutes.
4. Serve in a warm casserole dish garnished with chives, parsley, or other green herb and lemon wedges.

SERVES 4–6

Options: Add 1 tablespoon of shallots and a squeeze of lemon to scallops before broiling for a little more zing.

1½ pounds fresh bay scallops if available (October–February) or 1½ pounds fresh dry sea scallops

2 tablespoons butter, melted

Paprika

Chopped chives or parsley for garnish

The term "dry scallops" refers to scallops that have not been soaked in fresh water or a phosphate solution. Some fishermen and fishmongers soak scallops after the shucking process to increase the size and white the flesh. Scallops treated in this way will have a diminished flavor and will pop or spit when sautéed or broiled.

Smoked Scallops

½ gallon water

1 cup salt

1 tablespoon dried basil

2 bay leaves

1 tablespoon dried tarragon

1 tablespoon dried thyme

1½–2 pounds large sea scallops, halved horizontally

Chopped parsley, chives, or fresh dill for garnish

Though not found on many menus these days, there are few things better than a smoked scallop. The firm white flesh absorbs that wonderful smoky taste better than just about any other seafood. The combination of the firm texture, color, and smoky flavor will wow everyone. "Why haven't I had these before?" people will ask.

Smoking fish and seafood has the extra added bonus of being healthier than broiling or frying because you don't use any fats or oils in the cooking process. Stovetop smokers are available at most large kitchen retail stores and online. Larger models can be purchased at many outdoors and camping equipment suppliers. Be sure to follow the manufacturer's smoking instructions carefully for best results.

These morsels are best when served with individual dipping sauces. I recommend either dill sauce (page 190) or aioli (page 190).

1. Bring water, salt, and dried herbs to a boil. Remove from heat and refrigerate.
2. When brine is chilled, add scallops and return to refrigerator for 1 hour.
3. Rinse scallops and pat dry.
4. Place scallops on smoker rack and refrigerate overnight.
5. Place smoker rack in smoker and follow manufacturer's instructions.
6. Serve chilled, garnished with parsley, chives, or fresh dill, with lemon wedges and individually portioned dipping sauce.

SERVES 8–10

Scallop Ceviche

Ceviche (sometimes spelled seviche) is a South American coastal staple. Native versions often contain marinated raw fish, but American chefs use a wide variety of seafood. I often make it using a combination of fish, squid, and shellfish. Use what you like or what's freshest. That's the beauty of this dish—there is plenty of room for experimentation. The preparation is the same no matter what you use.

1. Remove side hinges from scallops.
2. Combine all ingredients except cilantro in a sealed glass or plastic container and refrigerate for at least 4–6 hours (overnight is preferred).
3. Serve in a martini glass or plate over a bed of greens and sprinkle with fresh chopped cilantro.

SERVES 4–6

1 pound bay scallops (whole) or sea scallops (halved)

⅓ cup lemon or lime juice

⅓ cup orange juice

⅓ cup diced red onions

¼ cup diced red peppers

¼ cup diced green peppers

¼ cup diced yellow peppers

1 teaspoon minced garlic

1 teaspoon red pepper flakes

¼ teaspoon white pepper

½ teaspoon salt

2 tablespoons extra-virgin olive oil

1 tablespoon cognac or brandy

1 tablespoon white vinegar

Coarsely chopped cilantro for garnish

Green Scallops

2 tablespoon butter

2 tablespoons minced shallots

½ cup white wine

¼ teaspoon salt

⅛ teaspoon white pepper

1 cup watercress, leaves only

1 cup heavy cream

4 diver scallops or 8 large sea
  scallops

Diver scallops have been hot on the culinary scene lately. This is a great recipe for these monster scallops. However, they can be somewhat hard to find. If diver scallops are not available, substitute with the largest sea scallops you can find.

To spice up the presentation, serve the scallops in scallop shells if they are available. Ask for shells at your local fish market.

1. Melt 1 tablespoon butter in a large nonstick frying pan over medium heat. Add shallots and sauté for 3 minutes.
2. Add white wine, salt, white pepper, and watercress and cook until liquid in pan has nearly evaporated. This should take about 5 minutes.
3. Add heavy cream and reduce by half.
4. In a separate pan, pan-sear scallops in 1 tablespoon butter over medium-high heat, 2 minutes on each side.
5. Serve on warm plates or in scallop shells topped with sauce.

SERVES 4

Option: Use spinach and Parmesan cheese instead of watercress.

Scallops Casino

The nice thing about casino butter is that is works well on just about any sea-food. As with any casino dish, you are going to want to present this one in shells. Since unshucked scallops are difficult to find, ask the kind people at your favorite fish market to save you some scallop shells. If you can't find scallop shells, individual ovenproof serving plates work nicely.

1. Preheat oven to 400°F.
2. Place one or more scallops, depending on size, on each shell. Add 1 heaping teaspoon of casino butter to each shell.
3. Place shells on a baking sheet. Bake for 10 minutes.
4. Serve on a warm plate, garnished with parsley and lemon wedges.

SERVES 4–6

¾–1 pound bay scallops or small sea scallops

Scallop shells

Casino butter (page 201)

Chopped flat-leaf parsley for garnish

Lemon wedges for garnish

Smoked Fish

Smoked Bluefish Pâté

1 pound smoked bluefish,
  roughly chopped

1 pound cream cheese, softened

¼ cup heavy cream

1 cup mayonnaise

Juice of 1 lime

2–3 drops Tabasco

3–4 drops Worcestershire sauce

¼ teaspoon liquid smoke

¼ teaspoon white pepper

½ teaspoon salt

For many years I smoked my own bluefish at the Home Port. The process was time-consuming but enjoyable. Sadly, there came a time when I couldn't do my own anymore. I just got too busy. But, as he had done so many times before, Louie Larson at the Net Result Fish Market came to the rescue, finding some wonderful bluefish smoked in Rhode Island that was every bit as good as the fish I did myself.

1. Place all the ingredients in an electric mixing bowl.
2. Using the paddle attachment, mix for 2 minutes on medium speed. Scrape the side of the bowl and mix for an additional 2–3 minutes or until mixture is smooth.
3. Serve on shredded or chopped lettuce (I learned this lesson the hard way). Garnish with black olives and serve with toasted crusty bread or crackers.

SERVES 6–8

I'll Have . . . Whatever That Is

Things were really rocking. It was a beautiful night. The sun was setting spectacularly, and we were booked solid. There was a line at the back door and not an inch of space on the patio. The staff was really rolling that night. Everything was going great until Alex, poor Alex, made one of the most legendary slipups in Home Port history.

The bluefish pâté is one of my favorite appetizers. It's a perfect mix of smoked bluefish and heavy cream to bring it all together. It's rich and creamy and smoky, and delicious spread over crackers or bread. The more decadent simply eat it with a spoon or their finger. It's that good. The problem with bluefish pâté—and pâtés in general—is that it can be a little slippery. Up until then we had presented it on a lettuce leaf. That all changed after poor Alex.

Alex came ripping out of the kitchen one night with a tray full of appetizers. As she rounded the corner into the dining room, the pâté slid off the plate like a hockey puck across freshly Zambonied ice. Normally, that wouldn't have been a problem. It certainly wasn't the first time someone lost a scoopful of pâté. Usually it slid harmlessly onto the floor in the kitchen, or off the plate onto the tray. Alex wasn't that lucky.

It was like in the movies, when things move in slow motion. This giant scoop of pâté went flying across the dining room and landed, splat! right at table 10. Table 10 is a four-top, and that night it was occupied by three impeccably dressed customers who had just been seated. Had it happened only minutes earlier, it wouldn't have been a problem. They didn't even have water or bread on the table yet, only their menus open in front of them. The scoop of pâté landed in the only empty seat, next to a gentleman, which would have been fine but for the creamy consistency of the pâté, which makes it so good. The second the airborne scoop hit the chair, it exploded—all over the walls and table and on the laps of the people at the table. All poor Alex could do was stand there looking horrified.

News of the catastrophe got back to me in the kitchen about the same time the pâté settled over everything. I went out immediately to smooth things over and see just how bad it was. It was everywhere. They were all very nice about it. I think they even felt a little bad for Alex, who was, by then, apologizing profusely. The gentleman, who I knew by the time the main course arrived would be smelling of smoked fish and spoiling cream, laughed a little and stuck his finger in a large glob of the pâté on the chair next to him and tasted it. "I'll have whatever that is," he said. The two women with him found that very delightful. We brought some out to the table, very carefully, and after that we started serving it over shredded lettuce.

Smoked Fish Dip

2 tablespoons chopped onion

2 tablespoons chopped celery

½ teaspoon chopped garlic

1 tablespoon butter

½ pound smoked salmon,
bluefish, or trout

½ cup mayonnaise

½ cup cream cheese, softened

½ cup sour cream

⅛ teaspoon liquid smoke

½ teaspoon dry dill

1. Sauté onion, celery, and garlic in butter over medium heat until transparent. Remove from heat and allow to cool for 15 minutes.

2. Combine sautéed vegetables with remaining ingredients in a food processor and blend until smooth. Refrigerate for at least 4 hours.

3. Serve with crackers or English cucumber slices.

SERVES 6–8

Smoked Marlin

Here is another opportunity to use that stovetop smoker. The finished product will have a texture more like a piece of beef than fish.

1. Bring water, salt, and herbs to a boil. Remove from heat and refrigerate immediately.
2. When brine is chilled, add fish and return to refrigerator for 1 hour.
3. Rinse fish and pat dry.
4. Place fish on smoker rack, cover, and refrigerate overnight.
5. Place rack in smoker and follow manufacturer's instructions.
6. Serve with dill sauce (page 190) and lemon wedges.

SERVES 8–10

½ gallon water
1 cup salt
1 tablespoon dried basil
2 bay leaves
1 tablespoon dried tarragon
1 tablespoon dried thyme
1½–2 pounds fresh marlin fillets, 1 inch thick

Then the fish came alive . . . and rose high out of the water showing all his great length and width and all his power and his beauty. He seemed to hang in the air above the old man in the skiff. Then he fell into the water with a crash that sent spray over the old man and over all of the skiff.

—Ernest Hemingway, The Old Man and the Sea

Fish and Crab

Codfish Cakes

1½ pounds fresh codfish, cut into 6–8 equal pieces

½ pound butter

⅓ cup minced onion

⅓ cup minced celery

2 tablespoons minced fresh garlic

1 teaspoon salt

1 teaspoon black pepper

1½ cups cold mashed potatoes

¼ teaspoon nutmeg

2 eggs, beaten

2 tablespoons roughly chopped fresh parsley

4 cups panko bread crumbs

5 tablespoons canola oil

This is one recipe where traditionalists might have cause to disagree with me: Traditionally, salt cod was the primary ingredient in codfish cakes. This was mostly out of necessity. Folks would have all this salted fish on hand for the long, cold New England winters, and cakes were one of the things they made with it. Thankfully, those days are long gone. When it comes to using fresh fish whenever possible, I'm happy to break tradition.

1. Melt ¼ pound butter in a large nonstick frying pan. Add codfish, onion, celery, garlic, salt, and pepper. Cook for 10 minutes over medium heat.
2. Drain frying pan through a colander with a large pot underneath to collect the liquids. Put drained liquids aside to make a fish stock later.
3. Transfer contents in colander to a large mixing bowl. Add mashed potatoes, nutmeg, eggs, and parsley and mix thoroughly.
4. Scoop out ⅓ cup of mixture and shape into a 1-inch-thick patty. Dredge patty in bread crumbs. Don't be afraid to use a little pressure to make bread crumbs stick.
5. Arrange cakes on a baking sheet lined with paper towels and refrigerate for 1–2 hours.
6. Remove from refrigerator and re-dredge cakes in bread crumbs.
7. Preheat oven to 350°F.
8. Heat 3 tablespoons butter and 3 tablespoons canola oil in a large nonstick frying pan over medium-high heat.
9. Sauté cakes until golden brown on both sides. Be careful not to crowd the pan. Repeat sauté process, adding more butter and oil as needed.

10. Arrange sautéed cakes on a new baking sheet (or remove paper towels from old one) and bake for 6–8 minutes or until crunchy.

11. Serve with tartar sauce (page 186) or aioli (page 190) and lemon wedges.

SERVES 6–8

Tuna Tartare

1 pound sushi-grade tuna, chopped into ¼-inch pieces

2 tablespoons minced shallots

2 tablespoons chopped fresh chives, cut into ¼-inch pieces

½ teaspoon lemon zest

1 tablespoon freshly squeezed lemon juice

2 tablespoons sesame oil

½ teaspoon salt

¼ teaspoon white pepper

1 English cucumber, sliced into ¼-inch-thick pieces

Throughout the years, broiled yellowfin tuna was one of our most popular "catches of the day." After I had cut the dinner portions from the 20- to 30-pound fillets, there would be some small pieces left over. Oh, darn. At the end of the night, my daughter Jessica, a New England Culinary Institute graduate, or my son Michael, a French Culinary Institute graduate, would be conscribed to make a little tartare as a treat for everyone. I'm borrowing this recipe from them.

Be sure the tuna is well chilled so it is easier to chop. Enjoy!

1. Place all the ingredients except cucumber slices in a large bowl and mix thoroughly.
2. Spoon tuna onto cucumber slices and serve on a cold plate.

SERVES 4–6

Options: Serve on crackers, toasted bread (crostini), potato chips, or the hood of your car for that matter. Try salmon instead of tuna. Use soy sauce, wasabi, or ginger and garlic for an Asian flavor. Go all out by topping it with caviar.

Crab Salad Lettuce Roll-Ups

As with any seafood recipe, the fresher the ingredients, the better it will taste. I recommend using only fresh crab for this dish because the other zesty ingredients may overpower crabmeat that is not fresh.

1. Combine all the ingredients in a bowl except for the carrots and lettuce.
2. Lay out lettuce leaves and place 3 or 4 carrot sticks on top.
3. Place a heaping tablespoon of crab salad on top of the carrots and roll up lettuce around scoop. Secure with toothpicks if necessary.

SERVES 4–6

1 pound fresh crabmeat

2 tablespoons mayonnaise

1 tablespoon creamy wasabi horseradish

Zest of 1 lime

Juice of 1 lime

2 tablespoons cilantro leaves, no stems

1 tablespoon chopped red bell pepper, cut into ¼-inch pieces

2 tablespoons coarsely chopped pickled ginger, drained

1 tablespoon capers, drained

Carrot sticks, sliced thin

Boston bibb or butter lettuce leaves

Crab Cakes

8 tablespoons butter

¼ cup minced shallots

1 pound lump crabmeat

¼ cup mayonnaise

1 teaspoon yellow mustard

6 drops Worcestershire sauce

1 egg, lightly beaten

1 teaspoon Old Bay or preferred
    seafood spice

¼ pound saltines, crushed
    (preferably in food processor)

8 tablespoons canola oil

Without a doubt, the best crab comes from Maryland, though you can get good crabmeat just about anywhere. Ask your local fish vendor for the best crab available for crab cakes. Personally, I like my crab cakes to be almost all crab. I want to really taste the sweetness of the crabmeat. Who cares if it falls apart on the plate?

1. Melt 1 tablespoon butter in a nonstick frying pan. Sauté shallots for 3 minutes over medium heat.
2. In a large mixing bowl, combine sautéed shallots, crabmeat, mayonnaise, mustard, Worcestershire sauce, egg, and Old Bay and mix gently.
3. Shape into 12–14 cakes. Dredge cakes in crushed crackers, pressing lightly.
4. Place cakes on a baking sheet and refrigerate for 2–4 hours.
5. In a large nonstick frying pan, melt 2 tablespoons butter and 2 tablespoons canola oil over medium heat.
6. Sauté cakes, flipping gently, until browned on both sides. Add more butter and oil as needed.
7. Serve with tartar sauce (page 186) or aioli (page 190) and lemon wedges.

SERVES 4–6

Options:

Add parsley, cilantro, dill, and minced green or red bell peppers to the mix.

French Crab Cakes: Add garlic and Provençal herbs.

Italian Crab Cakes: Add pepperoni, minced tomatoes, basil, and Italian spices.

Mexican Crab Cakes: Add minced jalapeños, hot sauce, minced chili peppers, minced red and green bell peppers, and minced onions.

Russian Crab Cakes: Add chopped potatoes, vodka, and minced red bell peppers.

Asian Crab Cakes: Add wasabi, seaweed, lemongrass, red curry paste, sesame seeds, and soy sauce.

Burning Down the House

Every year, right before the Home Port opened, we hosted the Chilmark volunteer fire department's annual cookout. It was always an enjoyable event to undertake: It served as a good test run for the season opening, and I figured it was never a bad thing to be in the fire department's good graces—though I prayed I'd never have to call upon those graces.

In 1993, the event was scheduled for the Saturday before Memorial Day, the day the restaurant opened for the season. Most of Friday was spent getting everything ready for the next day. It was late, probably pushing midnight, when I finished the last of the pies for the next day and went upstairs to bed. I had just drifted off when I heard the sirens. Menemsha is a small village, so when you hear sirens, you get up to see what's happening and help out however you can.

Turns out the fire department was coming to the Home Port—a day early.

The first thing I saw were flames shooting up from the old bunkhouse building. Thankfully, there was no one inside. It hadn't been a bunkhouse for nearly twenty years, and at that time housed a big walk-in freezer and industrial-size washer and dryer. The firemen managed to break the door down and get inside, and were horrified by what they saw. The gas line attached to the dryer had broken off and turned into a giant blowtorch. The next few minutes were probably some of the scariest of my life. Just past the building, which by that time was an inferno, was a 5,000-gallon propane tank that had just been filled the day before. If that went, the Home Port would have been nothing but a crater. Luckily, we were able to get the tank shut off before anything happened.

My son, Michael, was with me when it happened. He was just seven years old. I have never seen anyone as scared as he was. The look on his face is something I'll never forget. Some neighbors took him away from it all, calmed him down, and kept him for the night while we took care of everything.

It was a giant mess. The walls of the freezer had melted. I had just received a huge delivery the day before, and the freezer was practically overflowing with scallops and shrimp. After a couple hours of pumping water on everything, the firemen ran out of freshwater and started pumping saltwater out of the pond. By the time the sun came up, just about everything in the bunkhouse was ruined. Thankfully, the damage was restricted only to the bunkhouse. The restaurant remained virtually untouched.

Once the sun came up, I saw what a mess it was. Scallops and shrimp and ice cream and who knows what else oozed out of what was left of the freezer. The seagulls had a field day. There were hundreds of them over the charred remains of the old bunkhouse.

The gulls were fat that summer, fatter than I think I'd ever seen them. They turned out to be a great help in the cleanup, though, having pretty much picked it clean by the time we were able to get the tarps secured.

The firemen's dinner went on as scheduled. Fortunately, most of the prep had been done the day before and was safe in the walk-in inside. It was a big joke after that, how the fire department had to earn their dinner that year. I was lucky—very, very lucky—that was the extent of it. It could have been disastrous. I could have lost everything. I don't think I can ever thank everyone—the fire department and my neighbors—for all they did. Free lobsters and pie only goes so far. They saved my restaurant that night.

I will be forever grateful for their help.

Codfish pie (p. 127)

The Main Course

Boiled Lobster

Steamed Lobster

The Traditional Vineyard Clambake

The Shore Dinner at Home

Broiled Naked Lobster

Preparing Lobsters to be Baked and Stuffed

Baked Stuffed Lobster

Lobster Thermidor

Grilled Lobster

Lobster Salad

Lobster Sauté

Lobster Newberg

Broiled Swordfish

Grilled Swordfish

Teriyaki Swordfish

Swordfish Casserole

Broiled Salmon

Grilled Salmon

Poached Salmon

Pistachio-Encrusted Salmon

Asian Salmon

Broiled Cod

Baked Cod

Baked Cod with Lobster Sauce

Codfish Pie

Fried Haddock

Fin & Haddy

Haddock with Creamy Leeks

Broiled Striped Bass

Baked Striped Bass with Herb Stuffing

Steamed Whole Sea Bass

Baked Bluefish

Broiled Bluefish

Broiled Halibut with Mustard Glaze

Baked-Stuffed Sole with Lobster Sauce

Baked-Stuffed Sole with Spinach Sauce

Fried Sole

Baked-Stuffed Shrimp

Tropical Grilled Shrimp

Fried Shrimp

Shrimp Casserole

Shrimp Scampi

Shrimp Stir-Fry

Red Chili Shrimp

Shrimp Mac & Cheese

Broiled Scallops

Baked-Stuffed Scallops

Fried Scallops

Pan-Seared Scallops with Orange Sauce

Grilled Sea Scallops with Bacon and Vegetables

Sesame Tuna with Wasabi Butter

Grilled Marlin

Monkfish in Green Curry Sauce

Pan-Roasted Clams

Fried Clams

Stuffed Squid with Tomato Sauce

Calamari

Fried Soft-Shell Crab

Sautéed Soft-Shell Crab

Mussels with Pasta

Seafood Casserole

The Main Course

LOBSTER PRESENTATIONS

Without a doubt, lobster was the most popular item on the Home Port menu. We were, first and foremost, Martha's Vineyard lobster palace. During the high season (July and August), we sold anywhere between 300 and 400 lobsters a day. That's a lot of lobsters—straight off the boats that docked just a few hundred yards away.

Globally, the lobster industry nets around $32 billion annually, the vast majority of that based on New England lobster, the most well known and popular of the nearly fifty known varieties of the crustacean. Caught in the cold waters between Nova Scotia and New Jersey, New England lobster has become a delicacy due largely to the succulent flavor and firm meaty texture not found in other lobster varieties.

Ironically, lobster was not always considered a delicacy. Less than a hundred years ago, lobsters were considered a waste fish, suitable only for bait—or as sustenance by only the most desperate. To this day, Maine prisons are only allowed to serve lobster to convicts a limited number of times a week, a law put on the books after convicts rioted because they were forced to eat lobster too often. After fortifying their chowders with lobster, the poorest of the poor would sneak out late at night and bury the shells to escape the social stigma of having actually fed their families lobster. How things have changed.

Boiled Lobster

There's a reason the Home Port is called Martha's Vineyard's lobster palace. Our boiled lobster is, hands-down, the number one seller. There is a certain art to it but, as Chet Cummens said to me, "It's not rocket surgery."

If you live close enough to the ocean, boil your lobsters in seawater. It's the best way to boil a lobster. If that isn't an option, use 2 tablespoons of salt per gallon of water—it's the next best thing. Make sure you use enough water to completely cover all the lobsters.

Bring the water to a rolling boil before dropping in the lobsters. (No, that hissing sound isn't the lobsters screaming.) Boil 9 to 10 minutes for a 1-pound lobster, 12 minutes for a 2-pound lobster, 15 minutes for a 3- to 4-pound lobster. Once they have turned that beautiful red color, they are ready to go.

Serve with melted butter and lemon wedges, some crackers, and a bib—it will be needed.

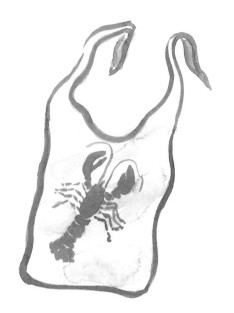

Steamed Lobster

In New England it's not uncommon to find kitchens equipped with a large enameled pot made specifically for steaming lobsters. A large pot with a rack placed on the bottom or even a perforated pie tin will also work just fine. All you need is 2 inches of water in the bottom, the lobster on top (out of the water), and the heat set on high. Cover the pot and let the steam go to work. When the lobster turns that beautiful red color, you are ready.

When steaming more than one at a time, be sure to rotate the lobsters on the top to the bottom after about 5 minutes. Use long tongs, and watch out for the steam. It can burn.

The Traditional Vineyard Clambake

48 cherrystone clams, scrubbed

10–12 pounds mussels, scrubbed and debearded

2–2½ pounds red potatoes, washed

12 ears corn, husk and silk removed

12 chicken thighs, marinated in barbecue sauce

1½ pounds sausage (linguica, chorizo, or Italian)

2 large onions, peeled and quartered

12 1- to 1¼-pound lobsters

1 pound butter

Lemon wedges

2 or 3 pies, blueberry, pecan, or other favorite flavor

If you're looking for a traditional Martha's Vineyard summertime experience, it doesn't get any more traditional than this.

1. When planning a clambake, the very first thing you need to do is pick out a stretch of sandy beach. After you have selected the ideal spot, make sure you are allowed to have a clambake there. Even on Martha's Vineyard, there are certain beaches that do not allow clambakes. Check with City Hall, the local police, or the Department of Natural Resources to make sure fires are allowed on the beach. There is nothing worse than lugging everything to the beach only to find out you have to move—or worse, having to pay a hefty fine.

2. Once you have a location lined up, make sure you have plenty of strong backs to help out. Put those strapping men (or women) to work and dig a 2 x 2 x 2-foot pit in the sand.

3. Line the pit with beach stones. I'm not talking boulders, but they need to be a decent size. You will usually need 20 to 30 to completely line the pit with a few left over to weight down the tarp.

4. Now make a raging fire in the pit—and I mean raging. You want a fire just short of epic proportions. Personally, I mix a little charcoal in with the wood because it produces more even coals than just wood and adds a little more flavor. Traditionalists might scoff at putting charcoal in the mix, but in the end, it's all about what works best for you.

5. Let the fire burn down to coals. If you build the fire correctly, it should take at least 2 hours.

6. After a nice dip in the ocean and a cold drink or two, start to get things ready. With the pieces of double-thick cheesecloth, make the following bundles: 4 bundles of cherrystones, 3 bundles of mussels, 3 bundles of potatoes, 3 bundles of corn, 3 bundles of chicken, and 2 bundles of sausage and onion.

7. Once you have a nice white-hot bed of coals, distribute them evenly over the bottom of the pit with a rake or shovel.

8. Lay about 8 inches of rockweed seaweed over the coals. Rockweed is the kind with the blisters, or sacks of water, on them. The water in these blisters helps steam the food and makes that wonderful popping and hissing sound. On the Vineyard, you can buy seaweed from various fish markets. Or, if you're feeling resourceful, it can be collected on the beach.

9. Lay the cheesecloth bundles over the bottom layer of the seaweed. Cover the bundles with a 2-inch layer of seaweed.

10. Place the lobsters on the second layer of seaweed. Cover the lobsters with a 4-inch layer of seaweed.

11. Soak the canvas or burlap in the ocean thoroughly and cover pit. Line the edges of the soaked canvas with rocks to prevent steam from escaping. Cook for 90 minutes.

12. With approximately 20 minutes remaining, put the butter in a saucepan and place on top of the canvas to melt.

13. Remove everything from the pit and serve with the melted butter and lemon wedges.

14. Now strap on that bib, pop open a cold one, and dig in. Be sure to leave room for some pie.

SERVES 10–12

What Else You'll Need:
Shovel

20–30 large sea stones or rocks

20–30 pieces of hardwood (enough for large fire)

Charcoal (optional)

18 pieces cheesecloth (double thickness), cut into 18 x 18-inch pieces

10 pounds rockweed seaweed

Large canvas tarp (at least 6 x 6 feet) or 4 or 5 large burlap sacks

Saucepan

Plates

Cups

Bibs (a dip in the sea afterwards works, too)

The Shore Dinner at Home

4 medium potatoes, halved

4 1- to 1¼-pound live lobsters

4 ears fresh corn

10–12 littleneck or cherrystone
    clams, scrubbed

4–5 pounds mussels, rinsed,
    scrubbed, and debearded

10 tablespoons butter, melted

Lemon wedges

Enjoy this Vineyard summertime tradition any time of year.

1. Using a lobster steamer or very large pot, bring 2–3 inches of water to a boil over high heat. Add potatoes and cover for 5–6 minutes.
2. Add lobsters, corn, clams, and mussels. Cover and continue to boil for 10–12 minutes. Check to see if the lobster is red and clams have opened. You may need to rotate items on the bottom to the top.
3. Continue to steam until lobsters are a beautiful red color.
4. Serve on a large warmed plate with melted butter and lemon wedges. Pour broth out of pot into individual cups for dipping clams and mussels.

SERVES 4

Options: Stuffed quahogs, broiled chicken quarters, spicy sausage, and steamed shrimp all go great with a shore dinner. Add what you like.

Big Bad John

One morning a few summers ago, I had to take our industrial dryer in to be fixed. That is one of the drawbacks of being on Martha's Vineyard: You don't just call for the repairman to come fix whatever is broken. And if you have ever been behind the scenes of a restaurant, there is always something broken, breaking, or just been repaired. To have the dryer down for more than a day or two bordered on catastrophic, not to mention costly, so it had to be fixed. When I called to have a repairman come fix the dryer, they said it would be at least a week before they could send someone over. My only alternative was to load it up and take it to them. So that's what I did. The repair shop was in Tiverton, Rhode Island, a couple hours away. Madeline and I drove down with the dryer and dropped it off, then went over to nearby Newport to kill time.

After a few hours, I called to check on the status of the dryer. Of course, it wasn't done yet, so we decided to take a harbor cruise. As we were pulling out of the harbor among all of the massive 120-foot mega-yachts, I happened to see one with *Big Bad John* on the stern.

For years Jimmy Dean—of breakfast sausage fame—was a familiar face at the Home Port. He would come in off his boat, *Big Bad John,* two or three times a year. At the time it was a 54-foot Bertram. His arrival was always an event. Word would get out that

he was coming, and we would go down and watch him bring his boat in. He was quite a boatsman. He didn't have a crew, like so many of the big boats that would come in. He crewed his own boat. He would stand on the flying bridge and wave to everyone as he came into the harbor. As he pulled her into the slip, he would turn around and work the wheel and the throttle behind his back. The Menemsha marina was pretty tight. Even professional captains sometimes had trouble maneuvering those big boats around. Not Jimmy—he made it look simple. It was pretty incredible to watch.

No sooner than he had the big boat tied off, Jimmy and his party—he always had a big party with him—would come up to the Home Port. He was tall and lanky, with a booming voice and slow Texas twang, just like in his commercials. He was always laughing. And everyone around him was always laughing, having what seemed to be the time of their lives.

It had been a couple years since we had seen Jimmy in the Home Port, and I wondered if the *Big Bad John* I saw tied up in Newport belonged to him. After the cruise I went over to the dock for a better look, on the off chance he might be there to say hello. With millions and millions of dollars worth of boats tied up, the security around those docks was pretty tight. I went down as far as I could. I could see the boat, but there was no way I was going to get to it. Just as we turned around to go, there was Jimmy Dean standing right there. I went over to introduce us, figuring he wouldn't know who I was out of the context of the Home Port. "I own the Home Port on Martha's Vineyard," I said. "I haven't been up to Menemsha since I got the new boat," he replied, with that languid drawl. "Can't get her in there."

Just then a stunningly attractive young woman walked out of a nearby T-shirt shop and came over. She was wearing a rock nearly the size of Kilimanjaro. "Now darlin'," Jimmy said to the woman who was obviously his wife, "I want you to meet Mr. Holtham and his wife, Madeline. They own that restaurant on Martha's Vineyard I've told you all about, with the best lobster in the world." He got very excited talking about it. And I have to say, his excitement was contagious. "We miss having you in," I said. And it was true. It was always a celebration when he came in to the Home Port, as I am sure it was everywhere he went. "Well, I guess I could drop a hook outside, couldn't I? Won't be able to make it up this trip, though," he said. "Right now I'm on my way down to Atlantic City. Seems Mr. Trump is kind of in trouble and he needs some of my money."

We talked and laughed for a while after that. He was truly a pleasure to talk to. Sure enough, right before we closed for the season that year, word came from the harbor master that *Big Bad John* had dropped anchor outside of the marina. I heard him at the front desk all the way in the kitchen—of course, he had a big party with him.

Broiled Naked Lobster

Don't have a lobster pot and want to serve whole lobster? No problem. Simply crank up your broiler. Ask for females when buying your lobster. For this dish, you are going to want females if at all possible for that delicious coral.

1. Preheat broiler.
2. Split lobsters and remove stomach and intestinal tract (see page 96). Leave in tamale and coral if female, tamale if male.
3. Place lobsters on a baking sheet and brush body cavity and tail with half of the melted butter. Cover with second baking sheet to keep lobster tails from curling while cooking.
4. Place in oven 6 inches from heat source. Broil lobsters for 5 minutes.
5. In a frying pan, mix garlic, shallots, thyme, lemon zest, and lemon juice with remaining butter. Heat for 3 minutes over medium heat.
6. Remove lobsters from broiler and brush liberally with the herb butter. Return to broiler for 5 minutes without top baking sheet.
7. Remove from heat and serve immediately on warm plates. Sprinkle parsley over lobsters, and serve with lemon wedges and melted butter.

SERVES 4

4 1- to 1¼-pound lobsters
(female if possible)

8 tablespoons butter, melted

2 garlic cloves, minced

2 medium shallots, minced

1½ teaspoons fresh thyme

Zest of 1 lemon

Juice of 1 lemon

Chopped flat-leaf parsley for garnish

Lemon wedges for garnish

Butter, melted, for dipping

Preparing Lobsters to Be Baked and Stuffed

1. Place a live lobster on its back on a large cutting board, with the head and claws facing away from you. Insert a large serrated knife in the middle of the lobster and cut down toward the head.

2. Turn the lobster around and cut from the starting point in its center down to the end of the tail meat. Do not cut the flipper.

3. Break the lobster body open to expose insides. In the cavity near the head will be a cloudy translucent stomach sack. Remove the stomach sack and discard.

4. Remove the intestinal tract that runs from the stomach sack to the tail and discard. Cook it up and enjoy. It's that simple. . . .

One Very Expensive Recipe

We were all in the lawyer's office getting ready to close on the Home Port. Chet and Esther Cummens came into the office and sat down. Esther had a bottle of champagne with her. The lawyer had all the papers ready to sign, and they couldn't sign them fast enough. Every August Chet would say, "I'd sell this place for the price of a bus ticket to Buffalo." It was a sentiment I often repeated over the years.

When we finished signing everything, Chet opened the bottle of champagne, sat back in his chair, and said, "You know, it wasn't the restaurant you just paid all that money for." I couldn't help but be a little confused by this comment. He chuckled, took a sip of his champagne, and said, "The restaurant is worthless. It's the baked-stuffed lobster and chowder recipes that are so valuable." We all had a good laugh over that one.

It took me years to tell him that the baked-stuffed lobster was one of the few things I changed my first year there. Chet's recipe had the tamale and the coral cooked off and added to the cracker meal. I left the coral and the tamale in the lobster and used a bread crumb stuffing with crab and lobster meat. My recipe had a little more texture to it, and it absorbed more butter.

Baked-Stuffed Lobster

When making the Home Port's number-two lobster dish, there is one thing to consider: The more butter and lobster meat you add to the stuffing, the better.

1. Preheat oven to 450°F.
2. Split lobsters down the middle. Remove stomach sack and intestinal tract (see page 96) and discard.
3. Remove the tamale and roe. If using tamale and roe in the stuffing, sauté in butter in a nonstick frying pan for 3 minutes over medium heat and put to the side.
4. Mix bread crumbs, lobster meat or crabmeat, Old Bay, and melted butter in a large bowl. Add tamale and roe if desired.
5. Fill lobster cavities with stuffing. Squeeze more stuffing in the palm of your hand and place down the middle of the lobster tail. Neatness counts with the presentation of this dish. Loose crumbs will burn.
6. Place lobsters on a baking sheet and cover with a second baking sheet (to keep tails from curling while cooking). Bake for 5 minutes on the middle rack.
7. Remove top baking sheet and continue cooking for 8–10 minutes until stuffing is golden brown.
8. Serve on warm plates. Garnish with lemon wedges, parsley, and butter for dipping.

SERVES 4

Options: Lemon zest, lemon juice, parsley, chives, cilantro, Italian spices, onions, peppers, and garlic and all make great additions to the basic stuffing recipe. Be creative.

4 1- to 1¼-pound lobsters

3 cups panko bread crumbs

8 ounces lobster meat or crabmeat

½ teaspoon Old Bay or preferred seafood spice

8–12 tablespoons butter, melted

Lemon wedges for garnish

Chopped flat-leaf parsley for garnish

Butter, melted, for dipping

Lobster Thermidor

4 1- to 1¼-pound lobsters or 1
   pound fresh lobster meat

6 tablespoons butter

½ pound mushrooms,
   quartered

½ cup chopped scallions
   (include green stalks)

1 teaspoon minced fresh garlic

¼ cup chopped roasted red
   peppers

1 teaspoon fresh thyme

½ teaspoon Old Bay or
   preferred seafood spice

2 tablespoons dry sherry

½ teaspoon Worcestershire
   sauce

1½ tablespoons flour

1 cup chicken stock

½ cup heavy cream

Salt and pepper to taste

½ cup grated Parmesan cheese

Chopped flat-leaf parsley for
   garnish

Put on your chef coat and hat for this oldie but goodie. This recipe requires a lot of ingredients, but don't be intimidated.

First you need to decide whether your thermidor will be made in individual ovenproof casserole dishes (the shortcut) or the more traditional way, in the lobster bodies. The recipe calls for 1- to 1¼-pound lobsters per person, but this is a good time to use culls (lobsters missing a claw). Five culls yield the same amount of meat as four regular lobsters—if not more. If you are serving the dish in-shell, try to find lobsters that are about the same size. If you are going the casserole dish route, I recommend 10-ounce au gratin dishes or ramekins. Using the casserole dishes eliminates the need to cook and pick the lobster meat, provided your fish market has fresh lobster meat available. If using lobster meat, you will need 6 to 8 ounces per person. The drawback to this is the price: Fresh lobster meat can run upwards of $50 a pound.

1. Boil lobsters for 4 minutes. Remove from water and allow to cool. Split lobsters and remove stomach sack and intestinal tract (see page 96). Remove claws and pick meat (leave tail meat intact).

2. Preheat oven to 400°F.

3. Melt 4 tablespoons butter in a nonstick frying pan. Add mushrooms and cook for 3 minutes over medium heat.

4. Add scallions, garlic, red peppers, thyme, Old Bay, sherry, and Worcestershire sauce and cook for 5 minutes.

5. Remove pan from heat. Add lobster meat and stir gently. Put to the side.

6. Melt remaining 2 tablespoons of butter in a saucepan over low heat. Add flour and stir continuously for 2 minutes.

7. Add chicken stock and heavy cream. Heat until thick and creamy.

8. Add lobster meat mixture to the saucepan and heat over medium-low heat for 2 minutes. Add salt and pepper to taste.

9. Divide ingredients into lobster bodies or casserole dishes. Place on a baking sheet and sprinkle with Parmesan cheese. Bake for 15 minutes.

10. Garnish with parsley and serve.

SERVES 4

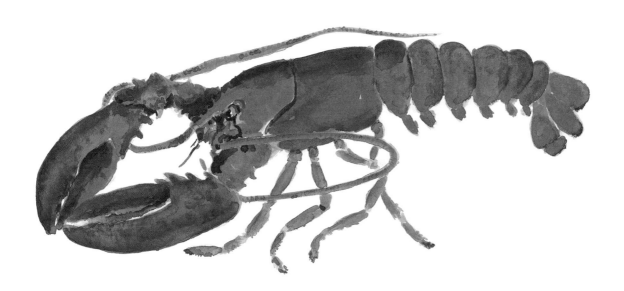

Grilled Lobster

3–4 teaspoons orange zest

½ cup orange juice

½ cup white wine vinegar

¾ cup ketchup

4 tablespoons red pepper sauce

4–6 drops liquid smoke

1¼ teaspoons salt

½ teaspoon sugar

½ cup extra-virgin olive oil

4 1- to 1¼-pound lobster

1 tablespoon chopped fresh
   basil leaves

Take your summer cookout to the next level with this wonderful recipe. And while you have the grill fired up, roast some whole ears of corn to go along with it. Since grilling can dry out lobster meat, boil the lobsters first and finish them up on the grill.

I provided this recipe to Vineyard Home & Garden *magazine a few years back. Served fresh off the grill or cold, it's great either way. The vinaigrette can be prepared ahead of time and kept in the refrigerator but should be room temperature when serving. Also, the lobsters can be boiled ahead of time and refrigerated.*

1. Place orange zest, orange juice, vinegar, ketchup, red pepper sauce, liquid smoke, salt, and sugar in a blender. Blend until smooth. Slowly add olive oil while continuing to blend.

2. Bring water to a boil in a lobster pot. Boil lobsters for 3 minutes.

3. Remove lobsters and allow to cool. Remove stomach and intestinal tract (see page 96).

4. If using a charcoal grill, make sure coals are hot. With gas, allow ample time to warm up.

5. Stir basil into vinaigrette. Brush lobsters tails with vinaigrette.

6. Grill lobsters for 3 minutes. Turn lobsters over, brush with vinaigrette, and cook for an additional 1–2 minutes.

7. Garnish with orange slices and basil sprigs. Serve with remaining vinaigrette and roasted corn on the cob.

SERVES 4

Lobster Salad

The best lobster salad is always made at home. This means boiling and picking the meat yourself. If you don't want to boil and pick lobsters, most fish markets have fresh lobster meat available. Unless it is your only option, try to avoid using frozen lobster meat. It just doesn't have the same taste as freshly picked. Use lobster culls. They are readily available and considerably cheaper than lobsters with both claws. Culls may be a little funny looking, but since you are picking the meat from them, no one is going to be the wiser. When dealing with culls, a 1-pound lobster generally yields 2½ ounces of lobster meat.

This recipe affords you the opportunity to really get creative with your garnishing technique. Experiment. Make it a work of art.

1. Chop lobster meat into bite-size pieces.
2. Mix all the ingredients except salad greens and vegetables in a large bowl. Add salt and pepper to taste.
3. Arrange salad greens on a chilled plate. Top with lobster salad and lightly drizzle dressing over everything.
4. Arrange vegetables on the side or add as part of plate presentation.

SERVES 4

8–10 pounds lobster culls or 4–6 ounces fresh lobster meat per person

¾ cup mayonnaise

¼ cup finely diced celery

1 tablespoon finely diced onion or shallot (optional)

1 tablespoon lemon juice

¼ cup vinaigrette or dressing of choice

Salt and white pepper to taste

Salad greens and your favorite fresh vegetables

Lobster Sauté

½ pound butter

4–6 ounces of fresh lobster meat per person

1 medium tomato (seeds removed), chopped into ½-inch pieces

2 scallions, chopped (include green stalks)

2 teaspoons dry sherry

Lemon wedges

This decadently rich meal is great for a special occasion and guaranteed to impress even the most finicky foodie. Again, you choose whether to boil and pick from live lobsters (use culls) or buy fresh lobster meat from the fish market.

1. Melt butter in a large nonstick frying pan over low heat. Add lobster meat and warm for 2 minutes, stirring occasionally. Remember the lobster meat is already cooked. Slow and low is the way to go with the heat.
2. Add tomato, scallions, and sherry. Turn up the heat to medium and cook for 1 minute.
3. Serve with lemon wedges on warm serving dishes.

SERVES 4

Options: Add Old Bay or other favorite spices to the mix. I have often served the lobster meat warmed in butter, placed into individual ovenproof casserole dishes, and topped with bread crumbs and spices. Heat in a 450°F oven until crumbs are light brown.

Flexing My Culinary Muscle

By the mid-1980s I had it in the back of my mind that I wanted to open a second restaurant, where I could do some of the things tradition prevented me from doing at the Home Port. Though I was able to implement a few subtle changes to the menu and the restaurant itself over the years, culinary-wise it would have been suicide to deviate much from Chet Cummens's formula. The traditions of the Home Port were bestowed upon me, and it was my honor, duty, and privilege to maintain those traditions and high standards: It's what people wanted and it's what people expected—demanded, actually—when they came to the Home Port. But after ten years of doing the same things, I was ready to flex my culinary muscle.

On an island full of history and fables, the story of the Square Rigger ranks right up there with the best of them. The building itself dates back to the turn of the 19th century, originally built on the dunes of the South Shore, where it served as both a residence and several businesses. As legend has it, one night the building was struck by lightning, killing an unfortunate soul inside. From then on the building was said to be haunted. Though I cannot verify the legend myself, there are plenty of people who claim to have seen the spirit of a man wandering the halls late at night, despite the building's repeated change in location.

The building was moved from the South Shore to Edgartown, where it served as several different businesses before it was moved again in the early '60s. The little wooden building was supposed to find a permanent resting place in Vineyard Haven, but it never quite made it.

Trippy Barnes, a legend on the island, was hired to move the itinerant edifice. It didn't matter that Trippy had never moved an entire building before. He was known for being able to do just about anything that needed to be done on the Island. If anyone was going to be able to move that place, it was going to be Trippy. Otherwise, someone from off-island would have had to come do it, significantly increasing the cost of moving the thing beyond what the owners of the building could afford. But just as Trippy was making his way out of town with the building, his trailer proved to be not quite up to the task and gave out. The building was moved onto a small island between two diverging roads, where it stayed, housing several businesses before it was turned into a restaurant, the Square Rigger, in the late '60s.

My first memory of the Square Rigger was when I worked for Chet Cummens. At the end of every season, Chet would take everyone who stayed to help clean up after the restaurant closed to dinner. The Square Rigger was one of the few places that remained open year-round. It was tiny, seating

The Square-Rigger Restaurant

Built about 1800 by Capt. Thomas Marshall Pease, who was a whaling captain and sailed square-rigged ships, the old house communicates a feeling of the Island in days long gone by.

The house has had many owners, the Thomas family and a Mr. Thomas Wilson of Boston, being among them. The original location of the house was at Edgartown Great Pond. Upon Mr. Wilson's death, the land was to be used as a bird sanctuary, the house was sold to Mr. Manuel S. Duarte of Vineyard Haven and moved to its present location by him.

The house was first used as an art studio and then as an upholstery shop. It has since been restored by Mr. John D. Donnelly, thus bringing to life, "THE SQUARE-RIGGER."

Most recently, Mr. Holtham, owner of the Home Port Restaurant in Menemsha, purchased the Square-Rigger and added the Open Hearth which the restaurant boasts today. The Square-Rigger now sails on, conveying traditional Edgartown hospitality and fine foods.

The history of the Square Rigger, printed on the back of the menu

maybe twenty people tops. The menu was small, featuring only five or six dishes, but each and every one of them was fantastic, including the signature dish, lobster Newberg.

Over the years they expanded the building as much as they could, and the restaurant evolved—or devolved, depending on who you ask—into more of a lounge than a restaurant. By the early '80s it was the place for locals to go for a drink or two. They would crowd in at night, six or seven deep at the bar. I would go and stand in line for a drink and marvel at the potential of the place. When John Donnelly, the owner, died, I made his sister, Anne, an offer on the place over lunch one day. By the time lunch was over, I had my second restaurant.

The Square Rigger was the culmination of all the restaurants I worked at over the years: the tradition of the Home Port, the aesthetics of Anthony's Pier 4's open-hearth kitchen, and the diversified menu of the Coach & Four, along with a million other little things from different places I enjoyed over the years. I made lobster Newberg the signature dish again, and offered different bouillabaisses (something I took from Pier 4) and some of the best steaks and chops on the Island. I wanted it to be more than just a seasonal place. There was a large enough permanent population in Edgartown to cater to the locals who lived there year-round. I offered several local specialties, like Fin & Haddy, a longtime favorite that could hardly be found anywhere anymore.

When I first began to contemplate opening a second restaurant, I knew from past experience (my own, and having watched some of the best restaurateurs in the world) that I couldn't do it without the right support staff. Some staffs are better than others. The restaurant business is, by nature, somewhat transient—particularly a seasonal restaurant like the Home Port. But at the time I had an incredible staff, one of my best ever, including Aram Berberian, who had worked for me every summer since he was twelve or thirteen, washing dishes standing on a milk crate. I wouldn't have been able to open the Square Rigger without him.

The Square Rigger was everything I hoped it would be. I enjoyed being able to offer things I couldn't do at the Home Port. It had a nice following, both local and seasonal. During the summer I still spent the majority of my time at the Home Port—the very nature of a restaurant like the Home Port demands more attention than a considerably less hectic place like the Square Rigger. With Aram running things, I knew the Square Rigger was in good hands. But after a few years, Aram decided he didn't want to stay in the restaurant business. He had worked hard to earn a college degree and decided he was ready to leave the Island and take it out for a test drive.

With Aram gone, the Square Rigger was taking up more of my time—time I couldn't necessarily devote during the summer months. An offer was made for it, and I took it. I really didn't want to give it up. I had put a lot of hard work into the Square Rigger and was very proud of what I had done. The Home Port was my loving and devoted wife, and the Square Rigger was my young and beautiful mistress: I knew where my place was—at the Home Port.

Superb employees like those pictured helped Will run the successful Square Rigger and Home Port restaurants.

Lobster Newberg

4 tablespoons butter

1 pound fresh lobster meat, cut into bite-size pieces

1 tablespoon lobster base

2 tablespoons flour

1 teaspoon paprika

1 tablespoon minced shallot

2 tablespoons dry sherry

1 cup heavy cream

3 egg yolks

2–3 drops Tabasco

3–4 drops Worcestershire sauce

Salt and white pepper to taste

This was a Square Rigger favorite and has always been a favorite of mine to make. It is kind of a tricky dish. The sauce is delicate and needs a lot of attention during preparation. It's worth the effort, though.

1. Melt butter in a large nonstick frying pan over medium heat. Add lobster meat and heat for 1 minute. Remove lobster meat and put to the side.
2. Add lobster base, flour, paprika, shallots, and sherry. Cook for 2 minutes over medium heat.
3. In a bowl, combine heavy cream and egg yolks and beat until smooth.
4. Add the cream and egg mixture to the frying pan along with Tabasco and Worcestershire sauce and wait for sauce to thicken. (If sauce becomes too thick, add additional cream.)
5. Return lobster meat to pan. Add salt and pepper to taste.
6. Serve in a puff pastry shell or over rice on a warm serving dish with toast points on the side.

SERVES 4

SWORDFISH

The Menemsha swordfish runs a close second in popularity to lobster at the Home Port. On any given day I would cut between 40 and 60 pounds of the magnificent beast—and not an ounce of it would be left at the end of the night. That's a lot of swordfish. Traditionally we served 14- to 16-ounce steaks, which, for all but the heartiest of appetites, would leave plenty left over. The supersized portions were a Home Port tradition, started by Chet Cummens, who would cackle with delight as he cut those incredible inch-and-a-half-thick steaks that flopped over the side of the plate. It is a tradition I continued.

When cooking swordfish at home, you have flexibility as to portion size, though there are few things better than a leftover swordfish sandwich with mayonnaise (add a little lime and cilantro to the mayo for some zing) or tartar sauce.

Buying swordfish can be a little tricky: Insist on fresh, not previously frozen. It can come from as far away as Chile, but when refrigerated and shipped properly, there is no discernable drop in quality. In July and August, keep an eye out for fresh-harpooned swordfish, often imported from Canada. It's hard to find and a little more expensive, but well worth it.

Simplicity is the key when preparing swordfish. Make sure your broiler or grill is as hot as it can get before cooking. Swordfish has both great flavor and texture when cooked properly. The high cooking temperature will make the outside of the fish firm while the inside remains tender and juicy.

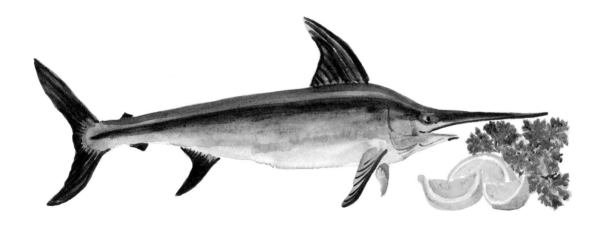

A Lost Art

Long before *Jaws* and Billy Joel and the Clintons and, ahem, the Home Port, Menemsha was known as a hotbed of swordfish fishing. The first few years I worked there, I remember the harbor filled with rickety old day boats, with towering flying bridges used for spotting the monstrous creatures sunning themselves in warm surface waters just off the coast of Martha's Vineyard. There were no massive 80-foot commercial fishing boats like they use to catch swordfish today. The boats then were relatively small—30 or 40 feet—and old; they showed their age and wear proudly, like floating badges of honor.

In the afternoons before I went to work, I would go down to the docks and watch these magnificent 450-pound creatures being offloaded from the boats. They would be hung up by the tail and weighed, and then taken straight to the fish market, where they would be cut up and brought over to the Home Port for dinner that night. The fish were still harpooned then, which was a terribly difficult and dangerous method of fishing. It was part sport, part art form. Sadly, that method of catching swordfish has been all but lost with the advent of commercial long-line fishing, which has resulted in the overfishing of the magnificent species. Now we only see one or two harpooned swordfish a year, and the fish they bring onto the docks are only about half the size they used to be.

The characters that went out every day in search of these elusive creatures were as colorful as they came. Many of them were bordering on insane. They would sneak up on the giant fish while they sunned themselves on the surface. Swordfish spend most of their time hunting in the vast darkness of the deep, deep water, where parasites attach themselves to the big fish's skin. To rid themselves of the parasites, the swordfish lie on the surface of the water and let the sun kill off the pests. On the surface, the fish could be spotted from the flying bridge of a boat, or even an airplane that buzzes the surface of the water and radios back the location of the fish. The boats would come along and harpoon the fish, and then the true test would begin.

The harpoons were attached to long lines with a buoy at the end. Often someone would go after the fish in a dory. Imagine being out in the middle of the Atlantic in a little wooden boat half the size of the fish it's attached to. It's very *Old Man and the Sea*. I used to hear these fantastic stories about how a fish would turn on the dory, attacking it with its sharp bill. The boats and the fishermen themselves had the scars to show for it. If you ever happen to be on the Vineyard, talk to anyone in the Larson family, the Tilton family, Everett Poole, or any of the Mayhew boys about their adventures. They aren't hard to find, and it's worth the time. For those of you unable to make it to the Vineyard to hear about harpoon fishing firsthand, books written on this lost art form number in the thousands.

The method of catching swordfish is very different today. It's called long-lining because 20 or 30 miles of baited line is put out in the water and left overnight. With this method they don't have to wait for the fish to come to the surface; they can go to the fish's hunting grounds and get them there. The best example of this is the book and movie *The Perfect Storm*. There is even a television show about it now. I think they depict the life of the long-lining fisherman pretty well. It's a terribly difficult existence. I can speak to that because I did it for a winter. I wouldn't say it made working hundred-hour weeks in a hot kitchen look easy, but it did give me a whole new appreciation for the fish I served up every night.

In the winter of 1979 I decided it was time for an adventure. I didn't quite know what to do with myself once the restaurant was closed for the season. There was only so much scalloping I could do. And to be honest, I needed it. My life had been the Home Port for the last two years. I had become friends with a lot of the local fishermen, many of whom long-lined in the winter, and one of them suggested I fish with his crew that winter. Personally, I think he just wanted to make sure his boat had a good cook. That was fine with me. I had tried to fish once before, a few years back, for tuna out of San Diego, and had been robbed of that experience by the Chilean government. I figured what the hell, sign me up.

We set out chasing the fish as they migrated south for the winter. We met bad weather off the Outer Banks of North Carolina: hurricane-force winds and 50-foot seas. I was convinced the steel hull of the boat was going to rip open like a bag of potato chips. I have never been so afraid in my life. Then the next day it all stopped and was perfectly calm. I watched the sun rise with the storm far off in the distance, dark against the light sky, and it was like the whole thing was just a bad dream and now I was awake. I understood that very moment why those fishermen did what they did for a living.

We steamed all the way down to the Gulf of Mexico. I spent my thirtieth birthday in Key West. Talk about a good time. We drank and chased women and fought anyone willing to take us on—typical fisherman stuff. But I have to say, I wasn't sorry when it was over. It was a once-in-a-lifetime experience, but not something I would ever want to do again.

Having seen how it works, it's pretty easy to understand how swordfish became overfished by the late '80s. With harpooning, the fish were caught one at a time, and they could gauge the size of the fish before harpooning them. They left the small ones alone, going only after those that had fully matured.

But with long-lining, there was no control over the size of the fish. Whatever size fish took the bait would be hooked. Because the lines were so long, 20 or 30 miles, it would take an incredibly long time to bring them in. Inevitably some of the fish on the lines would be dead, or eaten by sharks. I can't remember the number of times we brought up a half-eaten fish. There were all kinds of other things that would get caught on the lines as well, like sharks—lots of sharks. Occasionally we'd hook a turtle. They were massive creatures that would just as soon snap your arm off as look at you. They were protected, so we had to release them as quickly as possible.

Chet always preferred harpooned fish. He claimed he could tell from the color of the meat if a fish had been harpooned or long-lined. But he had the advantage of freshly harpooned fish every day. By the time I took over the Home Port, harpooned fish were becoming more and more rare. Thankfully, I have an incredible relationship with my local fish vendors. They know I only take the freshest sword-fish, so the quality hasn't suffered. Occasionally they do get harpooned fish, and we usually get one or two a year. We always let the customers know they are getting a real treat.

Broiled Swordfish

A Menemsha tradition and the Home Port's number-two seller.

1. Preheat broiler.
2. Melt enough butter to liberally brush both sides of the swordfish steak. And I mean liberally. Butter, butter, butter—that's the secret.
3. Squeeze lemon juice on both sides of the steak and sprinkle with salt, fresh cracked black pepper, and paprika or other preferred broiler spices. For a little more zip, try Cajun spice.
4. For swordfish steaks ¾ to 1 inch thick, broil for 4–5 minute on each side. Reduce time for smaller pieces.
5. Serve on a warm platter, garnished with lemon wedges and parsley.

SERVES 4

Options: The options for broiled and grilled swordfish are nearly limitless. The mild taste of the fish complements just about all sauces and marinades. When I marinate swordfish at home, I like it with a Thai glaze (page 200).

2–3 tablespoons butter

4 6–8-ounce swordfish steaks

Lemon wedges

Salt, pepper, and paprika, to taste

Chopped fresh flat-leaf parsley

Grilled Swordfish

When grilling swordfish, follow the broiling instructions on page 111. Make sure the grill is on high. Try not to turn the swordfish steaks more than once to keep uniform grill marks.

Teriyaki Swordfish

These easy-to-make morsels were created in the mid-'90s when our reservations were running nearly an hour late one particularly busy evening. I blame the sunset, which was so spectacular that everything came to a screeching halt. It happens sometimes. When we were running late like that, I liked to send out a little something for people to nibble on while they waited, compliments of the house, to say "We're sorry, and thank you for your patience." After the staff caught wind of how good these treats were, they became an all-time favorite after-shift snack. At the end of the night I would make up a big plateful, and they would be gone in seconds.

¼ cup soy sauce

2 teaspoons brown sugar

1 garlic clove, minced

1 teaspoon peeled and minced ginger

1 teaspoon dry sherry

¼ teaspoon red chili paste or 4–5 drops Tabasco

1 pound swordfish cut into 1-inch pieces

1 quart canola oil

Chopped fresh chives for garnish

1. Mix soy sauce, brown sugar, garlic, ginger, sherry, and chili paste in a large bowl.
2. Add swordfish pieces and stir gently. Cover and put in the refrigerator for 4–6 hours.
3. Heat oil in a heavy-bottomed pot to 350°F.
4. Strain swordfish from marinade. Cook for 2 minutes.
5. Garnish with chives and serve over rice.

SERVES 4

Swordfish Casserole

16–24 ounces swordfish pieces

1 tablespoon extra-virgin
olive oil

1 green pepper, julienned

1 red pepper, julienned

1 medium onion, julienned

2 garlic cloves, minced

1½ cups marinara

1 medium tomato, chopped

½ teaspoon Italian spices

Salt and fresh cracked black
pepper to taste

Chopped parsley for garnish

Here's a little tip: Ask your local fish market for swordfish pieces. These are the bits of juicy swordfish cut off when steak is cut to order at the market. Most fish markets keep these bits and pieces that are high grade but too small to sell individually. If your local fish market doesn't keep these pieces, ask them to. They come at a very good price and are perfect for dishes where the fish is not the center of presentation.

1. Preheat broiler.
2. Place swordfish pieces on a baking sheet and brush with olive oil.
3. Broil swordfish pieces for 2 minutes. Flip swordfish and continue broiling for another 2 minutes.
4. Set swordfish aside and turn on oven to bake at 400°F.
5. In a large bowl, mix the remaining ingredients (except parsley). Add broiled swordfish pieces and mix gently.
6. Pour mix into an ovenproof casserole dish, spreading evenly. Bake for 15 minutes.
7. Garnish with parsley and serve.

SERVES 4

Animal House

John Belushi and his wife, Judy, were Home Port regulars. He would always bring a crew in with him. Dan Ackroyd was there a lot in those days, as were Jane Curtin and others from the *Saturday Night Live* cast. On more than one occasion, Belushi would turn up in the Boston gossip columns having been spotted at the Home Port. This was before Martha's Vineyard became Hollywood East. I got to know Belushi over the few years he frequented the Home Port. Sometimes I would get a call right around closing time that he and some of his friends were hungry. I never had any problem staying open for them. I mean, really, having John Belushi and whoever he happened to have with him sitting in your restaurant hamming it up late into the night—who wouldn't jump at the opportunity for such a spectacle?

One night I remember quite vividly, probably because *Animal House* had just come out. Belushi and Ackroyd and some other people were there. They had actually come during business hours. The dining room was packed. Here was Belushi and his gang having a great time. Sitting across the restaurant was James Taylor. I don't remember who he was with, probably Carly Simon, his wife at the time, and some other music people. I'd have a hard time saying who was more famous at the time, Belushi or Taylor—it could have been Carly. Of course, they all knew each other. Martha's Vineyard is a small island.

We were cranking away in the kitchen when one of the waitresses came back. "They're on a roll tonight," she said. I poked my head out of the kitchen and saw Belushi and Ackroyd flicking their lemon seeds across the restaurant at James Taylor. When they extinguished their supply—and the supply of lemon seeds from the surrounding tables—Belushi eyed a piece of bread on the table. He picked it up and cocked back his arm like he was going to throw it. "Here it comes," I said to whoever was standing next to me, watching.

Part of me wanted to see it: I wanted to see John Belushi start a food fight with James Taylor. But at the same time, I had a dining room full of customers, the majority of whom would probably not see the humor of being hit upside the head with a lobster claw. It wouldn't have mattered if John Belushi had thrown it or not.

Just as he was about to hurl the piece of bread across the restaurant, John looked over to where I was standing and gave me one of his winks, and stuffed the entire piece of bread into a mouth already full of food. The Home Port did not become the Faber College cafeteria that night, but with hindsight being 20/20 and all, I wish it had.

SALMON

Most salmon found in fish markets these days is farm raised. Before we dammed up and polluted the major rivers in New England, wild Atlantic salmon was readily available. Environmental groups have done a good job getting the rivers cleaned up in the hope that Atlantic salmon will again return to their abandoned spawning grounds. There is, however, still a lot of work to be done. Farm-raised salmon provides a nice alternative at a reasonable price; however, I still prefer to pay a little more and use wild-caught whenever it is available.

Salmon is an incredibly nutritious fish, containing high amounts of protein and other essential nutrients. It is low in saturated fat and contains omega-3 fatty acids. Including a variety of fish in your diet can contribute to a longer life, and it's great for growing children as well. Start them early on salmon—they might like it. You don't even have to tell them it's good for them.

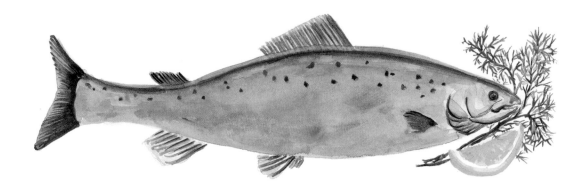

Broiled Salmon

Long before I came to own the Home Port, the restaurant was famous for its outrageous portions of the freshest possible seafood. This, surprise surprise, has carried over to the way I cook seafood at home. I love leftovers. Cold leftover salmon with a little red cocktail sauce (page 185) makes one hell of a good snack—and it doesn't hurt any that it's good for you. It will keep in the refrigerator for a couple days when stored properly.

1. Preheat broiler.
2. If using a whole salmon fillet, cut into 4 equal servings.
3. Place salmon on a buttered baking sheet skin-side down. Brush with melted butter. Unlike many of the broiled fish in this book, it doesn't need a whole lot of butter—just give it enough to give it a good coating.
4. Squeeze lemon over the top and sprinkle with paprika or other seafood seasoning.
5. Place in the middle rack of the oven and cook under the broiler for 5–6 minutes.
6. Turn heat off and let sit in the oven for an additional 2–3 minutes.
7. Serve on a warm plate and garnish with fresh dill and lemon wedges.

SERVES 4

Options: Broiled salmon is great on its own, but also goes wonderfully with ginger saffron sauce (page 191). Add a cup of jumbo lump crabmeat (that's crab with a c, not a k). The addition of color, taste, and texture will enhance the salmon threefold. Try serving it with a green vegetable. The green of the vegetable will set off the color of the salmon for a presentation guaranteed to make you look like a professional chef.

4 1½-inch-thick salmon steaks or 4 6-ounce fillets, or 1 1½-inch-thick whole salmon fillet, skin on

2–3 tablespoons butter, melted

1 lemon

Paprika or preferred seafood spice, to taste

Fresh dill for garnish

Lemon wedges for garnish

Grilled Salmon

4 1½-inch-thick salmon steaks
or 4 6-ounce fillets, or 1
2-pound salmon fillet, skin on

2 tablespoons extra-virgin
olive oil

Glaze of your choice

Salt and pepper to taste

Salmon fillets can be difficult to grill unless you have a fish basket or a fish grate. These two items are incredibly useful and inexpensive. They prevent the fish from sticking to the grill and falling apart while allowing you to enjoy the great flavor grilling adds to the salmon.

Sometimes I like to add a glaze to my grilled salmon for a change of pace. A ginger glaze (page 200) can really make the grilled flavor of the salmon pop. Don't have the time or ingredients to make a glaze? No problem. Creamy salad dressings are great, too.

1. Preheat grill to medium.
2. If using a whole salmon fillet, cut into 4 equal servings. Pat salmon dry with paper towel.
3. Brush fish grate and salmon with olive oil.
4. Place salmon on grate skin-side down (if using fillets). Brush on glaze. Salt and pepper to taste if desired.
5. Cover grill and cook for 8 minutes or until tops of fish begin to brown. Total cooking time will vary depending on thickness of salmon and temperature of grill.
6. Serve with a green vegetable.

SERVES 4

Poached Salmon

This is a great dish served either hot or cold.

1. Bring court bouillon to a boil in a 4-quart heavy-bottomed pot.
2. Reduce heat to a simmer. Add salmon fillets.
3. Simmer for 10 minutes for medium-rare, or longer for a more thorough cooking.
4. If serving hot, top with a dollop of butter and some dill. When eating cold (my favorite way to eat salmon), top with mayonnaise and capers or dill.

SERVES 4

2 quarts court bouillon
(page 184)

4 6-ounce salmon fillets,
skin on

Pistachio-Encrusted Salmon

1 cup whole pistachios, shelled

1½ pounds salmon fillets, skinless

¼ cup mayonnaise

2 tablespoons butter

2 tablespoons extra-virgin olive oil

Chopped parsley for garnish

Lemon wedges for garnish

As with most fish, adding different nut toppings will provide an endless variety of flavors. However, one of my favorite nuts to work with is the pistachio, simply because it is not used very often, despite being one of the most flavorful nuts available.

1. Heat a nonstick frying pan over medium heat. Add pistachios and brown, stirring frequently so as not to burn the nuts.
2. Remove pistachios from heat and let cool. When cooled, rub browned pistachios in a paper towel to remove dark skin from nuts.
3. Chop pistachios in a food processor using pulse mode or a nut chopper until finely chopped; however, a few large pieces won't hurt.
4. Cover flesh side of salmon with mayonnaise. Press nuts firmly onto fish.
5. Heat butter and olive oil in a large frying pan over medium heat.
6. Add salmon, nut-crusted side down, and sauté until light brown in color. Carefully turn over and sauté the other side for 3–4 minutes.
7. Remove salmon and place on a warm serving platter.
8. Before serving, garnish with parsley and lemon wedges.

SERVES 4

Asian Salmon

An hour or two in your favorite Asian marinade makes for a nice variation on any fish dish. I like to pan-fry salmon for this presentation, but grilling works well, too.

1. Marinate salmon fillets in glaze for 1 hour.
2. Place fillets in a large nonstick frying pan over medium heat. Cook for 3–4 minutes.
3. Flip and add more glaze if needed. Cook for an additional 3–4 minutes.
4. Remove salmon to a warm serving plate and pour pan juice over top.
5. Prior to serving, garnish with sesame seeds and chives.

SERVES 4

4 6-ounce salmon fillets

Thai glaze (page 200) or ginger glaze (page 200)

Toasted sesame seeds for garnish

Chopped fresh chives for garnish

WHITEFISH

Broiled Cod

The simplest way to prepare codfish is under a broiler. The secret here is to use plenty of butter, your favorite broiler spice, and a squeeze of fresh lemon.

Place the fish on a broiler pan (lined with foil for easy cleanup) and coat liberally—and I do mean liberally—with butter, spice, and lemon. Put the pan under the broiler and cook the fish until it is light brown in color. Turn the broiler off and move the pan down to the middle of the oven, and let cook for an additional 4 to 6 minutes, depending on the thickness of the fish. I always cook a little extra to enjoy cold with a squeeze of lemon and some red cocktail sauce (page 185).

As always, serve on a warm platter with lots of lemon. Enjoy!

Baked Cod

1. Preheat oven to 350°F.
2. Wash fillets and pat dry.
3. Place fillets on a greased baking pan and brush on melted butter. Squeeze lemon on fillets. Sprinkle with salt and pepper.
4. Top each fillet with a slice of onion and bacon. Sprinkle with paprika.
5. Loosely cover with aluminum foil and bake at 350°F for 15 minutes.
6. Remove foil and turn up heat to 450°F. Continue cooking for 6–8 minutes.
7. Serve fillets on warm plates, drizzled with juices from pan and garnished with parsley.

SERVES 4

4 6- to 8-ounce cod fillets

4 tablespoons butter, melted

Salt and pepper to taste

½ lemon

4 slices onion

4 slices bacon

Paprika

Coarsely chopped fresh flat-
  leaf parsley for garnish

Spelling Lessons

Scrod has long been a New England specialty. Yet, people can't seem to agree how to spell it. This little problem probably stems from the fact that it isn't a real fish. I've always spelled it scrod, so that's how I'll spell it here. However, the fish that isn't a fish can also be spelled schrod, as my mother found out one afternoon at a local restaurant.

My mother was perusing the menu at the popular Northeastern chain restaurant when she noticed what she thought was a typo and, being the consummate schoolteacher, felt obligated to bring it to the attention of the server. "Scrod isn't spelled with an *h*," my mother said. Confused, the waitress went back to check with the manager. "We get a lot of the seafood items on our menu from the famous Pier 4 restaurant in Boston," the waitress reported upon her return. "That's how they spell it." Without batting an eye my mother said, "Well, my son is the kitchen manager at Pier 4, and he never could spell."

Scrod, as it is generally known, can actually be one of three kinds of whitefish: small (less than 2½ pounds) codfish, haddock, or pollack. Codfish and haddock are essentially identical in taste and texture. Pollack is slightly different: Sometimes called Boston bluefish because of the slight bluish tint to the meat, it is usually larger than the other two fish and generally a little firmer. At the Home Port, our scrod is always codfish because, in my opinion, it's the best tasting and most versatile of the three: It's great baked, broiled, pan-fried, deep-fried, poached,

smoked, stuffed, and in chowders. I love it broiled and then chilled, served with a squeeze of lemon and red cocktail sauce, all wrapped in a lettuce leaf.

Because my scrod was actually codfish, I changed scrod to codfish on the menu a few years ago. That was a mistake. Sales dropped 50 percent. People wanted scrod. My waitstaff spent half their time trying to explain to people wanting scrod that the codfish was the scrod and vice versa. I changed it back the next year. However, in this book, I'll stick to calling the various types of fish by their proper names. You can call it—and spell it—any way you like.

Now, how these three different kinds of fish came to be known as the rather odd-sounding name scrod is as much a mystery as the type of fish you might get when ordering scrod. Some say it's an acronym for "**s**mall **c**od **r**emaining **o**n the **d**ock," while others say it means "piece cut off" in Dutch. Another version goes that a Victorian public house was advertising the "**s**pecial **c**atch **r**ecorded **o**n this **d**ay." The first and probably best story I've heard, however, is that the word was coined by Guy Perry, the longtime maître d' at the world-famous Parker House Hotel in Boston, giving the innocuous whitefish to be served that night a name so he didn't have to wait for the chef to return from the fish market before he wrote out the day's menu. There is probably some truth to all of these tales, and probably many more just like them.

Baked Cod with Lobster Sauce

4 6- to 8-ounce cod fillets

4 tablespoons butter, melted

1½ cups herb stuffing (page 203)

2 cups lobster sauce (page 192)

This was a special-request item at the Home Port. Though not on the menu, every year a few customers would want a little something to spice up their broiled scrod. We always had some of this topping mixed and ready, just in case.

1. Preheat oven to 400°F.
2. Place cod fillets on a greased baking pan. Brush with melted butter.
3. Place pan on top oven rack and bake for 2 minutes.
4. Remove from oven and top with herb stuffing.
5. Return pan to oven on middle rack. Cook for 10–12 minutes or until stuffing is golden brown.
6. Serve on a warm plate over lobster sauce. Drizzle pan juices on top of fish.

SERVES 4

Options: For a little something extra, add pieces of lobster, crab, scallops, or shrimp to the stuffing.

Codfish Pie

Yes, it might sound a little odd, but this fisherman's staple is damn good. Make enough to have some left over. In the morning, it makes a great breakfast. Trust me: It's delicious.

1. Bring water, bay leaves, and salt to a boil.
2. Poach codfish in the seasoned water for 3 minutes. Remove and let cool. Discard water.
3. Peel and boil potatoes until soft.
4. Add cream, 2 tablespoons butter, and salt and pepper to taste. Mash gently. Unlike Thanksgiving at your mother's house, lumps are fine and, in fact, encouraged. Let potatoes cool.
5. Preheat oven to 350°F.
6. Melt 2 tablespoons butter in a saucepan. Sauté mushrooms, onions, celery, and garlic over medium-low heat until celery becomes soft.
7. Coat a 6 x 9-inch au gratin or ovenproof casserole dish with butter. The dish should be at least 2 inches deep.
8. Cover the bottom of the dish with half of the mashed potatoes. Spread codfish evenly over layer of potatoes.
9. Cover fish with sautéed vegetables and frozen peas. Sprinkle cheddar cheese, thyme, and dill on top. Cover with remaining mashed potatoes.
10. Coat the top layer of mashed potatoes with bread crumbs followed by Parmesan cheese. Dot bread crumbs with dabs of the remaining butter. Add salt and pepper to taste.
11. Cover with aluminum foil and bake for 30 minutes.
12. Remove foil and broil to brown the top. Serve hot.

SERVES 4

Option: In the morning, shape leftovers into ½-inch-thick patties. Pan-fry and top with a fried or poached egg. Breakfast doesn't get much better than this.

1 cup water

4 bay leaves

2 teaspoons salt

1–1½ pounds codfish

6 medium potatoes (for mashing)

⅓ cup cream

8 tablespoons butter

Salt and pepper to taste

½ cup sliced mushrooms

¼ cup diced onion

¼ cup diced celery

2 garlic cloves, minced

⅓ cup frozen peas

¼ cup grated cheddar cheese

⅛ teaspoon thyme

¼ teaspoon dry dill

¼ cup bread crumbs

¼ cup grated Parmesan cheese

Fried Haddock

1 quart canola oil

½ teaspoon Old Bay or preferred seafood spice

1 cup flour

3 eggs

3 tablespoons milk

2 pounds fresh haddock, skin off, cut into 8 equal pieces

2 cups fine cracker meal or ¼ pound saltines, finely crushed

The Home Port's fish-and-chips was a back door favorite even before there was a Back Door. It is the quintessential take-out dish that harkens back to carefree summers on the Vineyard. At the Home Port, I always used haddock for my fish-and-chips because of its mild flavor and great texture when fried. Of course, any variety of scrod will work without a discernable difference in taste or presentation. This breading recipe can be used for all types of fish and seafood, including shrimp, scallops, oysters, sole, flounder, soft-shell crabs, calamari, and clams.

1. If you have a deep fryer at home, follow the manufacturer's instructions. If you don't have a fryer, don't worry. Use a heavy 4-quart or larger pot. Begin by heating oil to 360°F.
2. Mix Old Bay and flour in a large shallow bowl.
3. In a separate bowl, whisk eggs and milk together.
4. Dredge fish in flour mixture, shaking off the excess. Coat gently with egg wash and dredge in cracker meal. Make sure fish is entirely covered with the cracker meal.
5. When the fish is ready, test the oil temperature. When oil is 360°F, fry 4 pieces of fish at a time until they are golden brown.
6. Serve immediately with lemon wedges, malt vinegar, and tartar sauce. Please, please, please, whatever you do, make your own tartar sauce (page 186). The store-bought stuff doesn't do food this good justice.

SERVES 4

Fin & Haddy

You won't find this traditional Scottish favorite on many menus these days. It was one of my grandfather's favorites. Though smoked haddock might be hard to find, smoked codfish is readily available most anywhere and makes a perfect substitute.

Fin & Haddy was also a longtime standby at the Square Rigger when I was working for Chet Cummens. When I bought the Square Rigger, I put it back on the menu, for sentimental reasons more than anything else. It wasn't a big seller, but it did have a loyal following, including my friend Jeff Norton, who came in religiously once a week. Traditionalists serve it with buttery boiled potatoes and a green vegetable.

1. Place fish fillets in a glass baking dish. Fill the dish with milk so the fish is covered but still visible through the milk.
2. Place dish in a cold oven at 350°F for 30 minutes.
3. While the fish is cooking, melt butter in a saucepan over medium-low heat. Add flour and cook for 2 minutes, stirring slowly with a whisk.
4. Add bay leaves and half-and-half and continue to whisk slowly to prevent lumps. Cook until mixture is hot, thick, and creamy.
5. Microwave pearl onions for 1 minute and add to sauce. Add Worcestershire sauce and white pepper to taste.
6. Remove fish from oven and drain off milk.
7. Arrange fillets on a warm serving platter, cover with sauce, and garnish with chives.

SERVES 4

1–1½ pounds smoked haddock fillets, skinned and boned

1 quart milk

2 tablespoons butter

2 tablespoons flour

2 bay leaves

2 cups half-and-half

1 (16-ounce) bag pearl onions (thawed if frozen)

3–4 drops Worcestershire sauce

White pepper

Chopped chives for garnish

Haddock with Creamy Leeks

2 medium leeks

2 tablespoons butter

2 tablespoons extra-virgin olive oil

1½ pounds haddock, skin off, cut into 8 equal pieces

1 teaspoon minced garlic

Salt and pepper to taste

½ cup dry white wine

1 cup heavy cream

¼ cup chopped flat-leaf parsley (no stems) for garnish

This simple dish is huge on flavor and highly versatile. Though I usually prepare it with haddock, it is great with codfish, salmon, striped bass, flounder, grouper, small shrimp, small scallops, or any combination you choose.

1. Wash leeks in cold water and thinly slice, using only ½ inch of the green stem.
2. Heat butter and oil in a large nonstick frying pan. Sauté fish over medium heat for 2 minutes on each side. Remove fish and put to one side.
3. Reduce heat to medium-low. Mix garlic, leeks, a pinch of salt, and a pinch of pepper in frying pan and heat for 1 minute.
4. Add white wine and reduce by half.
5. Add cream and reduce until thick and creamy.
6. Return fish to pan. Cover and heat over medium-low heat for 2 minutes or until fish is warm.
7. Place fish on a warm serving patter. Spoon creamy leeks over fish and sprinkle with parsley.

SERVES 4

Broiled Striped Bass

This wonderful sport fish is celebrated every September on Martha's Vineyard with a bass derby that lures fishermen from around the world. Stripers, as fishermen in these parts know them, migrate with the cooling autumn waters from Maine to the Gulf of Mexico.

During the commercial fishing season in July and August, striped bass was more often than not the Home Port's Catch of the Day. Its firm, slightly flakey texture and mild flavor make it a suitable fish for a wide variety of presentations, though, in my opinion, it's hard to beat broiled, which is how it was most often served at the Home Port.

There are numerous glazes and sauces that complement broiled striped bass. My favorites are Thai glaze (page 200) and mustard glaze (page 199).

1. Preheat broiler.
2. Place fillets on a baking sheet, skin-side down. Brush liberally with melted butter and sprinkle with seasoning.
3. Place under the broiler until seasoning begins to brown. Remove from oven.
4. Set oven to bake at 400°F.
5. Once oven has cooled to 400°F, return fish to oven and bake for 8–10 minutes. Thicker pieces may take a little longer to cook through.
6. If adding glaze or sauce, brush on top of fish last 2 minutes of cooking.

SERVES 4

2 pounds striped bass fillets, skin on if available, cut into 4 equal pieces

½ cup melted butter

Old Bay or preferred seafood spice

Baked Striped Bass Topped with Herb Stuffing

2 pounds striped bass fillets, skin on if available, cut into 4 equal pieces

2 tablespoons butter, melted

Herb stuffing (page 203)

1. Preheat oven to 400°F.
2. Place fillets on a baking sheet, skin-side down. Brush liberally with melted butter.
3. Bake on middle rack for 5 minutes.
4. Remove from oven and cover fillets with herb stuffing.
5. Bake for an additional 8–10 minutes or until exposed fish is white and flaky. Use a fork to test the thickest portion of fillet. Don't be afraid to move the stuffing around to check. Just push the stuffing back over the fork hole. No one will ever know—and I certainly won't tell.
6. Serve on a warm platter.

SERVES 4

Option: For that little extra something, sprinkle Parmesan cheese on top.

Steamed Whole Sea Bass

Best known as tautog on Martha's Vineyard, Atlantic sea bass is also known as black sea bass or blackfish. It is smaller than its Pacific-dwelling cousin. Long a favorite in Chinese restaurants, it is often fried whole and presented eyes and all. Because of its firm texture, this fish is highly versatile and can be used in any recipe that calls for whitefish.

This recipe is the perfect opportunity to use that Chinese bamboo steamer collecting dust in the back of your cabinet. If you don't have one, they are relatively inexpensive and will prove to be very handy. You will also need a wok for this recipe. But should you find yourself not in possession of either of these items, do not despair: A roasting pan with a rack and cover will do the job more than adequately.

Complement the fish with individual dishes of dipping sauce. Tastes vary, so you may want to offer a variety. Personally, I like a Thai glaze (page 200).

1. Place 2–3 inches of water in a wok or roasting pan and bring to a boil.
2. Mix ginger, scallions, lemon slices, garlic, bay leaves, and cilantro in a large bowl.
3. Stuff as much of the mixture into the body cavity of the fish as you can without it spilling out. Spread the rest over the top of the fish.
4. Place the fish in the steamer or rack and cover. Let steam for 20 minutes.
5. For dipping sauce, mix soy sauce, brown sugar, vinegar, and sesame oil in a mixing bowl.
6. Serve on a warm platter. Garnish with extra cilantro, lemon wedges, and individual ramekins of dipping sauce.

SERVES 2–4

1 tablespoon thinly sliced fresh ginger

3–4 scallions, chopped (include green stalks)

1 lemon, thinly sliced

2 garlic cloves, thinly sliced

3 bay leaves

3–4 sprigs fresh cilantro, chopped, plus 3–4 whole sprigs for garnish

1 2- to 3-pound whole sea bass, cleaned and scaled

2 tablespoons soy sauce

1 tablespoon brown sugar

1 tablespoon red wine vinegar

2 tablespoons sesame oil

Steamed fish offers substantial health benefits over other methods of cooking.

Island Lure

In the late 1960s, any able-bodied young man faced the potential of being shipped off to fight in Vietnam. To avoid having their name pulled out of a hat, a few people I knew opted to enlist rather than leave their fates in the hands of lady luck. Two friends of mine from Granby, Mark and Billy, did just that, deciding they would probably be safer enlisting in the navy than in one of the other branches.

Before they were scheduled to report to boot camp, Mark and Billy took a rather lengthy road trip. They would call me at the Home Port and give me the sordid details of their trip. I was a little envious of the fun they were having. They made it all the way down to the Florida Keys and were coming back up the East Coast, seeing what there was to see along the way. They had some pretty incredible stories, all of which are not appropriate for this book. On their way back up, they decided to come see me on Martha's Vineyard. It was, I think, my second year working there, and I had spent a good amount of time regaling them with my own stories of drunken debauchery and scantily clad girls.

On their way, they stopped in Granby and picked up our friend Mike Lynch. He had just gotten back from a trip to Europe and was supposed to start college in the fall. Mike had a little time to kill, so he decided to come along.

I went down to meet Mark, Billy, and Mike at the ferry and we spent the day hanging out at the beach until I had to go to work. We met up later and I showed them how much fun the Vineyard was. They all seemed pleased they made the trip.

The next day, Mark and Billy dutifully called to check in with their recruiter, as they had been instructed to do every few days, and told him where they were. "You know damn well you're not allowed to leave the country!" the recruiter bellowed. Along with checking in, they were explicitly instructed to not leave the country. They tried to explain to him they were, in fact, still in the United States, but the recruiter wasn't buying it. This was back before Martha's Vineyard had been "discovered." Most people had never heard of it, including the recruiter. "Get back right now," the recruiter demanded. "You report tomorrow." Poor Mark and Billy had their trip cut short by more than a week. (Thankfully, they both came out of the war unscathed and are still close friends.)

When it came time for Mark and Billy to go, however, Mike wasn't quite ready. He had nothing but time on his hands. He didn't see why a navy recruiter's lack of geographical knowledge should spoil his fun. I knew Chet was in need of a dishwasher, so I talked to him about giving Mike the job. Mike went to work washing dishes that very afternoon—and he hasn't left the Vineyard since.

It happens quite often, actually. People come to the Vineyard for a vacation and fall in love with it, and never go back to wherever they came from. Mike spent the next few summers working at the Home Port. He came up through the Home Port system like the rest of us and knew the restaurant as well as I did. The fact that he fell in love with a

Successful Home Port romances. (Left to right) Katie Berberian, Julie and Aram Berberian; Jessica and Graeme Bradlee; John and Lassie Berellie; Heather and Sam Fischer; Mike and Pat Lynch; Leslie and Chris Neumann.

local might have had a little something to do with his staying as well. Pat Bennett was a waitress at the Home Port when he went to work there. They eventually got married.

Mike and Pat's romance was one of a couple dozen successful Home Port romances I have had the pleasure of witnessing over the years. When my daughter Jessica got married—another successful Home Port romance—we had the reception at the restaurant. People who worked there over the years, many of whom I hadn't seen in a while, showed up

to help us celebrate. During the reception I made an announcement that I wanted all of the successful Home Port romances to come down to the water for a picture. We started out and the next thing I knew, half of the people at the reception were following along behind us.

Mike is still on the Island. He owns a contracting company and has been a huge help to me over the years. With all the work we have done on the Home Port, it's as much his restaurant as mine. Well, almost.

BLUEFISH

Though fun to catch, many people find the flavor of bluefish a little overpowering. The strong flavor comes from the high oil content of the fish. The trick is to make sure the fish is immediately filleted and put on ice. This greatly reduces the strong flavor the oils in the fish generate when it is not immediately filleted. Because of the oily nature of bluefish, it is best when prepared with highly acidic items like lemons and tomatoes.

Baked Bluefish

4 tablespoons butter

2 1-pound bluefish fillets

2 lemons, cut into wedges

1 cup sliced onion

1 cup sliced green pepper

1 cup cherry tomatoes, halved

2 garlic cloves, thinly sliced

½ teaspoon Italian spices

Salt and pepper to taste

Chopped fresh parsley for garnish

1. Preheat oven to 350°F.
2. Grease a baking dish with approximately 2 tablespoons butter. Lay fillets in dish and squeeze half of the lemon wedges over fish.
3. Cover fish with remaining butter, onions, green peppers, tomatoes, garlic, Italian spices, salt and pepper to taste, and used lemon wedges. Cover with aluminum foil and bake for 20 minutes.
4. Remove aluminum foil and continue baking for 8–10 minutes or until fish begins to brown.
5. Remove to a warm serving plate and discard lemon wedges. Garnish with parsley and remaining fresh lemon wedges.

SERVES 4

Broiled Bluefish

1. Preheat broiler.
2. Place fish on a foil-lined baking sheet. Brush melted butter over fish and sprinkle with Old Bay.
3. Place fish 4–5 inches under broiler and cook for 4–5 minutes or until fish is light brown in color.
4. Turn off broiler, move pan to middle of oven, and continue to cook for 10–12 minutes, depending on the thickness of the fish.
5. Serve on a warm platter with lots of lemon wedges and garnished with parsley.

SERVES 4

Options: Spread mayonnaise, mustard, and fresh cracked black pepper over the fish before broiling. For a little zestier flavor, marinate fish in the following easy-to-make marinade.

2½–3 pounds bluefish fillets, skin on

3 tablespoons butter, melted

Old Bay or preferred seafood spice

Lemon wedges for garnish

Fresh parsley for garnish

Marinade for Broiled Bluefish

1. Mix all ingredients.
2. Baste bluefish in mixture and let sit for an hour or two before broiling.

3 tablespoons soy sauce

1 tablespoon brown sugar

2 garlic cloves, minced

2 tablespoons finely chopped onion

Juice of 1 lemon

½ teaspoon black pepper

FLATFISH

Go into any fish market, and you'll find enough different names of flatfish to fill a phone book. But the truth of the matter is that, for the most part, they are interchangeable: gray sole, winter flounder, summer flounder (sometimes known as fluke), yellowtail flounder, and sand dabs are all basically the same fish when cooked. Of course, they each have subtle differences in taste and texture, but nothing too resounding. My personal favorite is sole because it possesses a slightly firmer texture than the others, which allows it to hold its flavor a little better. Really, the only difference is size and the time of year the different fish are available. Halibut, the largest of the flounder family, is about the only one found year-round.

Broiled Halibut with Mustard Glaze

4 halibut steaks or fillets
1 lemon for juice
½ cup mustard glaze (page 199)
1 onion, thinly sliced
Chopped fresh parsley for garnish

This recipe works well with either halibut steaks (approximately 1 inch thick) or fillets.

1. Preheat broiler.
2. Wash and pat dry fish.
3. Arrange fish on a lightly oiled baking sheet. Squeeze lemon over fish, spread with mustard glaze, and top with onion slices.
4. Place fish 4–5 inches below broiler and cook for 6–8 minutes.
5. Turn off broiler and allow fish to continue to cook for 10 minutes.
6. Transfer fish to a warm serving plate. Garnish with parsley.

SERVES 4

Baked-Stuffed Sole with Lobster Sauce

This classic New England dish requires a little extra time to prepare, but it's definitely worth it. Either sole or flounder can be used—whichever is freshest at the market—though personally I prefer to use sole whenever I can.

2 cups panko bread crumbs

2 cups lobster sauce (page 192)

4 4- to 6-ounce sole fillets

Salt and white pepper to taste

2 cups milk

Chopped fresh parsley for garnish

1. Preheat oven to 400°F.
2. Combine bread crumbs and 1 cup lobster sauce in a large mixing bowl. Mix thoroughly and put to one side.
3. Cut each fillet in half lengthwise and sprinkle with salt and white pepper. Divide stuffing into 8 equal portions.
4. Roll one fillet around each portion of stuffing.
5. Place in a baking dish large enough to easily accommodate all 8 fillets. Add milk and cover dish with foil. Bake for 20 minutes.
6. While fish is cooking, reheat remaining lobster sauce.
7. Place cooked fish on a warm serving platter. Pour the sauce over the top of the fish and sprinkle with parsley.

SERVES 4

Baked-Stuffed Sole with Spinach Sauce

10 ounces fresh spinach

2 tablespoons butter

1 garlic clove, minced

2 tablespoons minced onion

1 cup heavy cream

Nutmeg

Salt

White pepper

4 6-ounce sole fillets

½ cup grated mild cheddar cheese

2 tablespoons grated Parmesan cheese

Though I prefer sole when it comes to flatfish, flounder also works well for this dish.

1. Preheat oven to 400°F.
2. Remove stems from spinach. Rinse spinach, chop roughly, and put to the side.
3. Melt butter in a large nonstick frying pan. Add garlic and onions and sauté for 3 minutes over medium-low heat.
4. Add spinach, heavy cream, and pinches of nutmeg, salt, and pepper. Cook over medium heat, stirring occasionally until cream has reduced by half.
5. Remove from heat and pour half of the spinach mixture into a baking dish suitable for presentation.
6. Place fillets over the spinach mixture. Cover fillets with remaining mixture and sprinkle with cheddar and Parmesan cheese.
7. Bake for 15–20 minutes or until top is light brown.

SERVES 4

Options: Top with bread crumbs and dabs of butter. Add cooked bacon pieces to spinach. Add a pinch of tarragon as a complementary taste to the spinach.

Fried Sole

We always include a piece of fried sole on our fish platter, along with shrimp, scallops, and oysters. When I fry up a batch of sole, I always make a little extra because it's absolutely delicious left over with a squeeze of lemon and a little red cocktail sauce (page 185). The only secret here is to make sure your frying oil is hot (360°F is the ideal temperature) and let the fish sit for a minute on paper towels to absorb the excess oil.

1. If you have a deep fryer at home, follow the manufacturer's instructions. If you don't have a fryer, use a heavy 4-quart or larger pot. Begin by heating oil to 360°F.
2. Mix Old Bay and flour in a large shallow bowl.
3. In a separate bowl, whisk eggs and milk together.
4. Dredge fish in flour mixture, shaking off the excess. Coat gently with egg wash and dredge in cracker meal. Make sure fish is entirely covered with cracker meal. Press firmly.
5. When the fish is ready, test the oil temperature. When oil is 360°F, fry fish until they are golden brown.
6. Remove to paper towels. Season with salt and pepper to taste.
7. Serve immediately, with lemon wedges, malt vinegar, and tartar sauce (page 186).

SERVES 4

1 quart canola oil

½ teaspoon Old Bay or preferred seafood spice

1 cup flour

3 eggs

3 tablespoons milk

2 pounds fresh sole, skin off, cut into 8 equal pieces

2 cups fine cracker meal or ¼ pound saltine crackers, finely crushed

Salt and pepper to taste

SHRIMP

America's favorite seafood, shrimp has always been a big seller at the Home Port. On any given day, we usually served around 40 to 50 pounds of shrimp. That's a lot of shrimp. However, due to our location, shrimp was the only seafood I would ever even consider buying frozen.

In more southern latitudes, fresh shrimp is readily available. In the warm waters of the Atlantic and Gulf of Mexico, they grow plump and sweet, and are great for just about everything, from shrimp cocktail to boils and gumbos. However, the cold Atlantic waters, which are so good for so many seafood species, just don't produce good shrimp. It is worth mentioning that Maine does have a winter harvest of wild shrimp running January through April. These shrimp are small (often used for popcorn shrimp), usually 80 to 100 per pound. However, the majority of shrimp available at northern fish markets are previously frozen, farm-raised varieties, usually from Vietnam or Thailand. Farm-raised shrimp have the same nice texture as wild shrimp but since they are generally raised in freshwater ponds, they lack some of the sweetness found in wild shrimp.

Sold by the pound, the general rule is the larger the shrimp, the more it will cost per pound. They can range from 2 or 3 shrimp to nearly 300 per pound, so you have a wide range to choose from size-wise. Most recipes call for a certain size of shrimp, but the nice thing about these tasty buggers is you have a lot of leeway at the fish market. If you are looking to save a couple bucks, buy smaller shrimp. You will have to make more, but will still save a little cash in the long run.

It's a sin to overcook shrimp, and like so many sinful things, it's easy to do. Overcooked shrimp becomes tough and loses the fabulous texture and sweetness it is known for. Be vigilant when cooking shrimp. As soon as it turns that beautiful pink color, it's done. Simple as that!

The Home Opener

Hershel West was a regular fixture at the Home Port for just about as long as anyone can remember. We lovingly referred to him as the Mayor of Menemsha because he knew everyone and everything about the village. He was one of the last true Crickers around— as native as they come. When I worked for Chet Cummens, Hershel would stop in all the time. It didn't matter if we were open or not. He would just come to the back door and Chet or I would make him something to eat, and he would sit and chat. When I took over the Home Port, that didn't change. My first year as owner, he was a fixture in the kitchen during the lonely months I spent there before I opened for the season. The day before the big opening, he came by and I made us a couple of lobster salad sandwiches. We sat at a table in the dining room, and he talked for a long time about how the place had changed over the years. "See you tomorrow," he called out as he walked toward the docks, his little black poodle yapping at his heels.

Opening day was really exciting. There was a buzz on the Island. We were booked solid. People wanted to see how much I would change things, I think. I had sworn up and down in the newspapers, and to anyone who would listen, that nothing would change. Well, almost nothing—I did change the baked-stuffed lobster recipe, but nothing else, and I doubted if anyone would notice. Other than that, it was still very much Chet's restaurant. But because I had worked there before, and a lot of people knew me, I think they gave me the benefit of the doubt. The flower delivery guy and I became good friends that day. People sent huge bouquets of flowers, wishing me well. By the time we were ready to open, the place looked like a flower show. I didn't have room for all the flowers people sent.

About an hour before we were set to open, Hershel showed up at the back door. He had on clean clothes and had left his omnipresent ball cap that sat cocked a little crooked on the top of his head back on his boat, and what was left of his hair was combed. He smiled at me and said, "I'm hungry." I put him at the best table in the house and he looked approvingly at the menu—the same menu Chet had used the year before. He ordered the baked-stuffed shrimp. I went back to the kitchen and went to work on the first official meal I prepared as owner of the Home Port. He finished just as the first reservations of the night were starting to show up. I went out and asked him what he thought. "Not bad," he said with a big grin on his face. That was the best compliment I could get that night.

When we opened the next year, there was Hershel, waiting to be the first customer of the season. He had the baked-stuffed shrimp again. When he finished, I asked him how it was. "Not bad," he said. Every year after that he continued to be the first customer served on opening day. He always had the baked-stuffed shrimp, and every year when I asked him how it was, he said, "Not bad." In thirty-two years he only missed one opening night. He was working a salvage job about 20 miles offshore and got socked in by some bad weather. I still made the baked-stuffed shrimp and we served it at his table, just like he was there. I didn't want to jinx anything.

Baked-stuffed shrimp

Baked-Stuffed Shrimp

About fifteen years ago, I was forced to change my recipe due to political problems in South America. The original recipe called for jumbo (10 count) shrimp. The shrimp we got was wild from a couple places in South America, and it was really high quality. But it seemed some rebels decided they didn't want their local shrimp industry prospering like it was. (Maybe someone didn't pay off somebody they were supposed to. It's hard to say.) The rebels blew up the shrimp factories, sending the already high demand for the shrimp through the roof. Prices more than doubled, if the shrimp was available at all. I was forced to use a slightly smaller, farm-raised shrimp (16 count) from Asia. Jumbo shrimp is more readily available today, but the price remains very high.

4 cups panko bread crumbs

4 ounces lobster meat or crabmeat

6 tablespoons butter, melted

½ teaspoon Old Bay or preferred seafood spice

1½ pounds (12–15 count) shrimp, peeled, deveined, and butterflied (split down the middle)

1. Preheat oven to 450°F.
2. Mix bread crumbs, lobster meat or crabmeat, melted butter, and Old Bay in a bowl (for a more spicy flavor, use more seafood seasoning to taste).
3. Place 3 tablespoons of stuffing in your hand and compress (kind of like an elongated snowball). Press stuffing in butterflied shrimp and space on a flat baking sheet.
4. Bake for 6–7 minutes or until stuffing turns golden brown.
5. Serve immediately on warm plates.

SERVES 4

Options: Shallots, garlic, parsley, and other herbs can be added to the stuffing. Experiment. See what you like best.

Tropical Grilled Shrimp

¼ cup chopped green pepper

¼ cup chopped red pepper

⅓ cup chopped onion

1½ tablespoons chopped garlic

1½ tablespoons peeled and chopped fresh ginger

2 small jalapeños, chopped

1 cup unsweetened coconut milk

3 tablespoons lemon or lime juice

1 teaspoon salt

½ teaspoon white pepper

3–4 sprigs cilantro

1½ pounds shrimp (16–20 count), peeled and deveined

4 tablespoons butter, melted

There are several ways to grill shrimp. Grill pans make it easy. Skewering them is another option, as is just tossing them on the barbie, as the Aussies like to say. Really, it doesn't much matter how you do it.

I recommend marinating shrimp for a couple hours beforehand to soak up some flavor. This coconut-based marinade is one of my favorites. If you're not a fan of coconut, try a ginger glaze (page 200) or Thai glaze (page 200), or any of your favorite marinades. Remember, shrimp are very lean and will need to be basted several times as they cook.

1. Mix all the ingredients except shrimp and butter in a food processor for 15 to 20 seconds. Do not puree.
2. Put shrimp and marinade in a sealable container or freezer bag and refrigerate for no longer than 2 hours.
3. Heat grill to 450°–500°F.
4. Place shrimp on the grill and cover. Keep in mind the shrimp will only need to cook 2–3 minutes per side.
5. Turn and baste with melted butter. Cook for an additional 2–3 minutes or until shrimp is pinkish white.

SERVES 4

Options: Wrap shrimp in ham or blanched bacon.

Fried Shrimp

My mouth waters at the very thought of fried shrimp. Probably my favorite way to eat fried shrimp (or any fried seafood for that matter) is topped with a squeeze of fresh lemon and dipped in melted butter. It may be a heart attack waiting to happen, but it's delicious all the same. Should you not have your cardiologist on speed dial, there are the old standbys like tartar sauce (page 186) and red cocktail sauce (page 185). I know I keep saying it, but please, please, please, *whatever you do, don't use the store-bought stuff. Take the five minutes to make your own. It's time well spent. For a little more exotic flavor, whip up a green cocktail sauce (page 186), aioli (page 190), or cilantro sauce (page 187). And don't forget the lemon.*

1 quart canola oil

½ teaspoon Old Bay or preferred seafood spice

1 cup flour

3 eggs

3 tablespoons milk

1½ pounds shrimp (16–20 count), peeled and deveined

2 cups fine cracker meal or ¼ pound saltines, finely crushed

1. If you have a deep fryer at home, follow the manufacturer's instructions. If you don't have a fryer, use a heavy 4-quart or larger pot. Begin by heating oil to 360°F.
2. Mix Old Bay and flour in a shallow bowl.
3. In a separate bowl, whisk eggs and milk together.
4. Dredge shrimp in flour mixture, shaking off the excess. Coat shrimp gently with egg wash and dredge in cracker meal. Make sure shrimp are entirely covered with the cracker meal.
5. Test the oil temperature. When oil has reached 360°F, drop those beauties in carefully and pluck them out as soon as they are golden brown.

SERVES 4

Be sure to keep one hand for the dry ingredients and one for the egg wash; otherwise your fingers will have more breading than the seafood.

Shrimp Casserole

5 strips bacon, cut into ½-inch pieces

½ cup minced shallots

¼ cup minced celery

2 garlic cloves, minced

4 tablespoons butter

1½ pounds shrimp (16–20 count), peeled and deveined, tails off

2 cups coarsely chopped fresh spinach, packed firmly, no stems

½ cup coarsely chopped fresh parsley, leaves only

½ lemon for juice and zest

1 cup shredded Asiago cheese

½ teaspoon Tabasco

½ teaspoon Worcestershire sauce

2 tablespoons flour

1½ cups heavy cream

1 tablespoon lobster base

½ teaspoon Old Bay or favorite seafood spice

½ cup panko bread crumbs

½ cup grated Parmesan cheese

Feel free to substitute lobster, crab, or poached scallops for shrimp in this recipe. A combination of two or three different kinds of seafood also works nicely.

1. Fry bacon in a nonstick frying pan until crisp. Remove bacon from pan and set to the side.

2. Place shallots, celery, garlic, and 2 tablespoons butter in the same pan and sauté for 3 minutes over medium-low heat.

3. Remove contents of pan to a mixing bowl and add shrimp, spinach, parsley, lemon juice and zest, bacon pieces, Asiago cheese, Tabasco, and Worcestershire sauce, and mix together.

4. Generously butter an ovenproof casserole dish suitable for table presentation. Place shrimp mixture in the dish.

5. Preheat oven to 375°F.

6. Melt 1½ tablespoons butter in a heavy saucepan over medium-low heat. Add flour and cook for 4 minutes, stirring frequently.

7. Warm heavy cream and add to the saucepan. Add lobster base and Old Bay. Cook on medium-low heat until sauce is thick and creamy.

8. Pour sauce over shrimp mixture in casserole dish. Sprinkle with bread crumbs and Parmesan cheese.

9. Bake for 30–35 minutes or until top starts to bubble and turns golden brown.

SERVES 4–6

Shrimp Scampi

1. Melt butter in a large nonstick frying pan over low heat. Add garlic and cook for 3 minutes, stirring frequently. Be careful not to burn the garlic.
2. Add shrimp, Italian spices, lemon juice, and sherry. Turn up heat to medium and cook until the shrimp are pink on both sides.
3. Remove from heat. Add basil and parsley and stir.
4. Serve over pasta or rice.

SERVES 4

Option: Use scallops instead of shrimp.

6 tablespoons butter

1 tablespoon minced garlic

1 pound shrimp (16–20 count), peeled and deveined

½ teaspoon Italian spices

2 teaspoons fresh lemon juice

1 teaspoon dry sherry

2 tablespoons chopped fresh basil

1 tablespoon chopped fresh parsley

Shrimp Stir-Fry

3 tablespoons sesame oil

1½ pounds shrimp (16–20 count), peeled and deveined

2 teaspoons minced fresh garlic

2 teaspoons peeled and minced fresh ginger

1 green pepper, julienned

1 red pepper, julienned

1 medium onion, julienned

2 carrots, peeled and julienned

1 cup snow pea pods

½ cup sliced water chestnuts (use a whole cup if you like them)

3 tablespoons soy sauce

½ cup hoisin sauce

1 lime for zest and juice

Salt and pepper to taste

⅓ cup cilantro, leaves only

I have always loved Asian flavors, so when I opened the Square Rigger, I put this dish on the menu. Customers had the choice of shrimp, lobster, or scallops. Shrimp was the most popular, but feel free to substitute or combine whatever you prefer. This is best prepared in a wok over high heat, but a large nonstick frying pan will also work nicely. Have all of the ingredients prepared and ready, because once the wok (or frying pan) is hot and the oil is smoking, it all comes together quickly.

1. Place a wok (or large frying pan) on stove burner over high heat. Heat 2 tablespoons oil. Spread oil over sides of wok.
2. Add shrimp and cook for 90 seconds, stirring occasionally. Remove shrimp and put to one side.
3. Add 1 tablespoon oil, garlic, and ginger to wok and cook for 15–20 seconds.
4. Add peppers and onions and cook for 1 minute.
5. Add all remaining ingredients except shrimp, salt and pepper, and cilantro and cook for 2 minutes, stirring occasionally.
6. Add shrimp and cook for 1 minute.
7. Serve in a warm bowl over rice. Add salt and pepper to taste and sprinkle with cilantro.

SERVES 4

Options: Add sliced Chinese cabbage, broccoli, cauliflower, mushrooms, or bean sprouts. For a little extra heat, add red chili paste.

Red Chili Shrimp

This delicious recipe is for those who like their seafood on the spicy side. It can be prepared as a main course over rice or as an appetizer with cilantro sauce (page 187) for dipping.

1. Heat butter and olive oil in a large saucepan over medium heat. Add chilies and garlic and sauté for 90 seconds.
2. Add shrimp and paprika. Sauté until shrimp turn pink (3 to 4 minutes), stirring frequently.
3. Squeeze lime over top and salt to taste. Serve immediately.

SERVES 4

Option: For a little more heat, add Sriracha Hot Chili Sauce to taste.

2 tablespoons butter

2 tablespoons extra-virgin olive oil

2 tablespoons finely chopped fresh red chilies (leave seeds in for extra heat)

4 garlic cloves, finely chopped

1½ pounds shrimp (16–20 count), peeled and deveined

1 tablespoon paprika

1 lime, halved

Salt to taste

Shrimp Mac & Cheese

2½ cups elbow macaroni

8 tablespoons butter

¼ cup minced onion

2 tablespoons flour

2 cups milk

2–3 bay leaves

¼ teaspoon Old Bay or preferred seafood spice

2 chicken bouillon cubes

2½ cups grated sharp cheddar cheese

1 pound shrimp (16–20 count), peeled and deveined

½ cup panko bread crumbs

¼ cup grated Parmesan cheese

You can never go wrong with this easy-to-make dish. Even the kids will like it. I frequently serve it as a main course, but it works well as a side dish, too.

1. Add macaroni to salted boiling water. Cook for 8–10 minutes, stirring occasionally, until macaroni is tender. Strain macaroni and put in a large bowl.
2. Add 2 tablespoons butter to pasta, mix, and put to the side.
3. Melt 3 tablespoons butter in a nonstick saucepan. Add onions and sauté for 2 minutes over medium heat, stirring occasionally.
4. Add flour. Reduce heat to medium-low and cook for 2 minutes, stirring often.
5. Preheat oven to 350°F.
6. Warm milk in microwave for 1 minute.
7. Add warm milk, bay leaves, Old Bay, and chicken bouillon to saucepan. Cook over medium heat for 2 minutes, stirring frequently with a whisk.
8. Add cheddar cheese and simmer for 2 minutes, stirring frequently.
9. Add shrimp and cook for 2 minutes.
10. Pour cheese and shrimp sauce over macaroni. Mix thoroughly. (Add extra milk if sauce mixed with macaroni is too stiff.)
11. Pour into a well-buttered ovenproof casserole dish suitable for table presentation. Sprinkle with bread crumbs and Parmesan cheese. Add dabs of butter.
12. Bake for 25–30 minutes or until the top is golden brown.

SERVES 4

Options: Substitute shrimp with lobster, crab, or lightly poached scallops. Garnish with fresh parsley or scallions.

SCALLOPS

If scallops are the crown jewels of seafood, then Cape Cod bay scallops are the diamonds of all scallops. We're lucky here on Martha's Vineyard: The elusive little buggers are gathered literally just outside our doors. They are the sweetest and richest tasting of the different varieties of scallops. They are also fragile—plentiful one year, only to all but vanish the next—and incredibly time consuming to gather, process, and store, which is why their prices can be so high. Cape Cod bay scallops are also smaller than other, more prevalent varieties, ranging from 60 to 90 scallops per pound. But they are certainly worth it. Don't fret: You won't have to break the bank for these delectable treats.

The scallops most people are familiar with are sea scallops. They are larger than the scallops caught in the ponds and lagoons around Martha's Vineyard, averaging between 20 to 60 per pound, but can come as big as 5 or 6 per pound. They are gathered from the continental shelf from Iceland to the Gulf of Mexico. I prefer a midsize scallop, 30 to 40 per pound, for most recipes. The biggest advantage of the sea scallop over the bay scallop is availability. Bay scallops are only available fresh during late fall and early winter. That means having to freeze the local scallops when they are caught for the next season. Fresh sea scallops, however, are available year-round.

The third type of scallop commonly seen is the calico scallop. This is the smallest variety of scallop. Gathered in warmer, southern waters from Georgia to the Gulf of Mexico, calico scallops average more than 90 per pound, are very white in color, and have less flavor—they are, therefore, the least expensive. These are best suited for use in stews and chowders.

When purchasing scallops from a fish market, be sure to ask for fresh "dry" scallops. Dry scallops have not been previously soaked in freshwater to increase their size. Soaking whitens the color and dilutes the flavor, and makes them pop when cooked.

Like all seafood, I prefer to undercook scallops slightly to preserve the delicate flavor. Overcooking dries out seafood and makes it tough—and no one likes dry, tough seafood.

The best thing about scallops is their versatility. They can be used as the center of a dish and combine well with other seafoods, vegetables, and pastas. They can be baked, broiled, grilled, sautéed, deep-fried, poached, stuffed, smoked, and my personal favorite, eaten raw.

Old-Timer

I was in the kitchen prepping for the night when the hostess came in with a rather perplexed look on her face. She had the reservation book in her hand and held it up for me to see that we were booked solid. "A Mr. Cagney is on the phone and says he would like his usual table for tonight," she said. "James Cagney?" I asked. "I think so. We're booked solid," she replied, somewhat incredulously. It was her job, as much as anything, to turn people away. She was always very sweet about it. "Put him at table 20 whenever he wants," I told her. She looked at me, puzzled, knowing there were only a handful of people who could call and get a table when we were booked—and even they didn't get table 20. It was the best table in the house, right in the corner with an incredible view of the water. "Okay," she said hesitantly. She started to turn to go back to the office and stopped halfway: "Who's James Cagney?"

James Cagney had been coming to the Home Port for nearly as long as it had been open. He first landed on Martha's Vineyard in the mid-'30s, at the height of his career, buying Holly Farm, a spectacular 70-acre estate surrounded by stone walls that backed onto the water. He said he bought it because there weren't any paved roads around for miles. Well, over the years that changed, but his place never did. He and his wife lived in the same drafty little clapboard farmhouse that was on the property when he bought it. Mr. Cagney was a very private man. It was said he had armed guards posted around his property to keep people away. Whether that's true or not is hard to say.

Mr. Cagney was one of the first celebrities to spend large amounts of time on the Vineyard. When I first started working at the Home Port, I remember how excited I was when I heard he was coming to dinner. I hate to admit it, but I even found an excuse to sneak out of the kitchen and catch a glimpse of him. It was *the* James Cagney, all right. He was older and a little rounder, but he didn't look all that much different. And as soon as I heard him speak, I knew it was him for sure. He was with his wife and a few of his gang, none of whom I recognized right away but am sure were people I should have known.

I always heard the stories of the people who would come to visit him: Gary Cooper, Humphrey Bogart, Charlton Heston, Frank Sinatra, Fred Astaire, Cary Grant—the Hollywood elite of the '30s and '40s. According to one of the more popular Island tales, Spencer Tracy came to visit him and was either late or early—I've heard it both ways. Mr. Cagney wasn't at the ferry to meet Mr. Tracy, so he took a cab. About a mile or so from Cagney's house, the cab driver stopped and refused to get any closer. "I hear they shoot," the cabbie told Tracy. "You're walking from here."

I have to admit I was more than a little disappointed to learn Mr. Cagney was a steak man. He always ordered the chopped sirloin. I wanted to say I cooked James Cagney a lobster. Over the years I had plenty of opportunities to cook for him, and it was always a thrill to do so for icons like him. Only once, in all the times he came in, can I remember him ordering anything other than beef. He ordered the broiled scallops, and I was sure it was a mistake. I asked the waitress if she was positive that's what he wanted. She had been there for ages and was one of my best waitresses, and had waited on him probably two dozen times over the years. She was just as surprised as I was. I made him the broiled scallops and hoped to get out and ask him how they were, but we were very busy and by the time I had the chance, he was gone.

This Home Port classic tempted confirmed beef-lover and longtime Home Port regular James Cagney.

Broiled Scallops

1½ pounds fresh sea scallops

2–3 tablespoons butter, melted

Paprika, Old Bay, or preferred
    seafood spice

Salt and black pepper

Lemon wedges

This is one of the more popular entrees at the Home Port: simple to prepare, delicious, and elegant. I use butter, but extra-virgin olive oil works well if you are a little more health conscious.

1. Preheat broiler.
2. Pat scallops dry with a paper towel.
3. Place scallops on a heavy sheet pan and brush on melted butter. Sprinkle with paprika, salt, and pepper.
4. Place under broiler for 2 minutes or until paprika starts to darken. If scallops are large, they may need to be turned over, re-seasoned, and cooked for 1 more minute or until firm. Do not overcook.
5. Serve with lemon wedges.

SERVES 4

Baked-Stuffed Scallops

1. Preheat oven to 400°F.
2. Place scallops in an ovenproof casserole dish. Brush liberally with butter and cover with stuffing.
3. Cover casserole dish with foil and bake for 10 minutes.
4. Remove foil and continue to bake for 8–10 minutes or until stuffing is golden brown.

SERVES 4

Option: Cover scallops with provolone cheese before applying the stuffing.

1½ pounds sea scallops
2 tablespoons butter, melted
Herb stuffing (page 203)

Fried Scallops

1 quart canola oil

½ teaspoon Old Bay or preferred seafood spice

1 cup flour

3 eggs

3 tablespoons milk

1½ pounds sea scallops (30–40 count if available; larger scallops will need to be cut in half)

2 cups fine cracker meal or ¼ pound saltines, finely crushed

I used to think bay scallops were the best for frying, but bay scallops have a rich, sweet flavor that is more suited to simpler preparations. The flavor of sea scallops is a little more briny and tastes more like the ocean—that's what you're looking for in a fried scallop.

1. If you have a deep fryer at home, follow the manufacturer's instructions. If you don't have a fryer, use a heavy 4-quart or larger pot. Begin by heating oil to 360°F.
2. Mix Old Bay and flour in a shallow bowl.
3. In a separate bowl, whisk eggs and milk together.
4. Dredge scallops in flour mixture, shaking off the excess. Coat gently with egg wash and dredge in cracker meal. Make sure scallops are entirely covered with the cracker meal.
5. Fry scallops until they are golden brown. Do not crowd pot.
6. Serve immediately with lemon wedges and tartar sauce. Please, please, please, whatever you do, make your own tartar sauce (page 186).

SERVES 4

Pan-Seared Scallops with Orange Sauce

The first time I had these, I was at a tapas bar in Florida. It seems like they put orange juice in everything down there. It doesn't always work out, but in this case, wow! *This is best suited as a main course, but it works well as an appetizer, too.*

1. Mix flour and Old Bay. Dredge scallops in flour mixture. Shake off excess.
2. Heat butter and olive oil in a large nonstick frying pan over high heat. Once the butter and oil are hot, add the scallops and sear on one side for approximately 2 minutes or until golden brown.
3. Turn scallops over and cook for 1 minute.
4. Mix garlic, ginger, orange juice, sour cream, white wine, honey, and tarragon in a bowl.
5. Pour mixture over scallops and cook for 2 minutes over medium heat.
6. Transfer to a warm serving plate. Garnish with parsley sprigs.

SERVES 4

1 cup flour

1 tablespoon Old Bay or preferred seafood spice

1½ pounds sea scallops

2 tablespoons butter

2 tablespoons extra-virgin olive oil

1 tablespoon crushed fresh garlic

1 tablespoon peeled and grated fresh ginger

¼ cup orange juice concentrate

1 cup sour cream

¼ cup white wine

1 tablespoon honey

2 tablespoons chopped fresh tarragon leaves, cut into ¼-inch pieces

Parsley sprigs for garnish

Grilled Sea Scallops with Bacon and Vegetables

¼ cup sesame oil

¼ cup soy sauce

¼ cup orange juice

1 tablespoon minced fresh garlic

1 tablespoon brown sugar

½ teaspoon black pepper

1½ pounds sea scallops

20 cherry tomatoes

1 large onion, julienned

1 green bell pepper, julienned

2 portobello mushrooms, sliced

2 yellow summer squashes, sliced

6 thick slices bacon, cut into 1-inch pieces

Lemon wedges, parsley, and chives for garnish

To properly prepare this recipe, you are going to need a grill pan. The high heat and smoke of the grill give the scallops and vegetables that wonderful caramelized (a word used way too often in cooking circles these days, but in this case apt) texture.

1. Place sesame oil, soy sauce, orange juice, garlic, brown sugar, and black pepper in a large bowl and whisk together.
2. Pour marinade into a sealable freezer bag. Add all remaining ingredients except bacon and garnishes and refrigerate for 1 hour.
3. Heat grill and grill pan.
4. Drain scallops and vegetables from marinade in a bowl. Save marinade.
5. Cook bacon on grill pan for 2 minutes.
6. Add scallops and vegetables. Cook for 3 minutes, stir, and cook for another 3 minutes. Place on a warm serving plate.
7. Heat marinade in a saucepan and pour over serving plate. Garnish with lemon wedges, parsley, and chives.

SERVES 4

Marinated and grilled, these scallops and vegetables are the perfect foil to crisp, smoky bacon.

Some Good Advice

It was a terrible day to be out scalloping. It was freezing cold and rainy, with gale-force winds blowing everything sideways. I was miserable, to the point of questioning my own sanity. Did I really need to be out doing this? I was still new at it, and really struggling. And the weather wasn't helping any. There were a lot of scallopers out there, though. I figured they knew something I didn't—something I wanted to know. So I was out there, slogging through it. And, I must say, rather unsuccessfully.

As I chugged through the choppy water, the wind and rain at my face, everyone out there looked at me a little funny when I went past them. They would shake their heads and mutter something to themselves as they went the other way. After watching me struggle for a few miserable hours, Donald Poole finally pulled his little boat up alongside mine. Donald was a true bear of a man who spent his entire life fishing, with massive shoulders and no discernable neck, gruff and coarse, a fisherman through and through. He was the patriarch of the Poole fish market empire on the Island.

Donald made the very task with which I was struggling so mightily look quite easy. He had a smaller boat with a smaller engine than mine, yet he seemed to have no problem cutting through the rough water. When he pulled alongside me, I saw his culling board was overflowing with scallops. I, on the other hand, after several miserable hours, had gathered less than a dozen, including the ones I had eaten. "Son," he said to me with his gruff Martha's Vineyard accent, "never do what the wind will do for you."

That was some of the best advice I have ever received. And I think only a little of it had to do with scalloping.

1 tablespoon sesame seeds

1 tablespoon wasabi powder

2 tablespoons butter, softened

4 6-ounce tuna steaks, 1 inch thick

3 tablespoons sesame oil

2 teaspoons freshly ground black pepper

Fresh cilantro leaves for garnish

Sesame Tuna with Wasabi Butter

When I was growing up, the only tuna most people knew about came from a can. Not so anymore. Fresh tuna has become an incredibly popular item, prepared in hundreds of different ways. Yellowfin, or ahi, is probably the most popular. Bluefin is considered a delicacy in Asia and is often shipped there. For this recipe, I recommend yellowfin or bluefin, though albacore is a good substitute if it is the freshest.

1. Place sesame seeds in a nonstick frying pan and toast over medium-low heat, stirring frequently so seeds do not burn. When light brown, remove from heat and put to one side.
2. Mix wasabi powder with 1 tablespoon water. Stir into softened butter and refrigerate.
3. Preheat a cast-iron skillet or heavy-bottomed frying pan over high heat until skillet is very hot. While skillet is heating, rub the tuna with sesame oil and black pepper.
4. Place tuna in the skillet and cook for 1 minute on each side. If steaks are thinner than 1 inch, cook for a little less time. Be careful not to overcook.
5. Remove from pan onto a warm plate. Place a piece of wasabi butter on top of each steak and sprinkle with toasted sesame seeds and cilantro.

SERVES 4

Grilled Marlin

Marlin is not always easy to find but is certainly worth the effort. You usually will have to have it special ordered from your local fish market. In texture, marlin closely resembled beef, making it easier than some fish to prepare, but provides the many health benefits of fish. It varies in color depending on where it was caught: East Coast marlin tends to be more pink, while West Coast marlin generally has more of a creamy color.

Simple preparation doesn't mean losing out on flavor. This simple marinade will enhance this mild-tasting fish that is similar to swordfish but with a meatier texture. I recommend serving marlin medium-rare. It goes great with grilled vegetables.

¼ cup extra-virgin olive oil

4 garlic cloves, crushed

1 lime, halved

2 tablespoons grated onion

2 tablespoons soy sauce

½ teaspoon salt

½ teaspoon crushed fresh black pepper

1 tablespoon light brown sugar

4 6-ounce marlin steaks, 1 inch thick

1. Mix olive oil, garlic, juice of half lime, onion, soy sauce, salt, pepper, and sugar in a large bowl.
2. Place marlin in a large sealable freezer bag and cover with marinade. Allow fish to marinate at room temperature for 2–3 hours.
3. Place on a hot grill. Squeeze some lime over top of fish.
4. Cook for 3 minutes on each side (for medium-rare). Squeeze more lime over the top of fish after flipping.

SERVES 4

Monkfish in Green Curry Sauce

1 tablespoon extra-virgin
   olive oil

½ red pepper, julienned

½ green pepper, julienned

2 garlic cloves, minced

1 tablespoon green curry paste

1¾ cups coconut milk

1½ pounds monkfish, cut into
   2-inch pieces

Salt and pepper to taste

Fresh cilantro leaves for
   garnish

2 scallions, chopped, for
   garnish

In the summer of 1977, I was sent around the corner to Poole's Fish Market to pick up something for Chet Cummens, then the owner of the Home Port. Everett Poole was busy filleting some fresh monkfish when I got there. Monkfish are an odd-looking fish, all head and teeth. I had never seen a whole monkfish before. Standing there watching him fillet this prehistoric-looking beast, I completely forgot what I was there to get. When Everett asked me what I wanted, I told him I completely forgot. "Take this back," he said, lopping the head off one particularly scary-looking fish and skinning it for me. He explained how monkfish is one of the most underutilized fish in America. Most of it, in fact, is shipped to France. I took this now wonderful-looking piece of whitefish to the restaurant. Chet didn't say a word about what I was supposed to bring back.

Monkfish is still one of my favorite kinds of fish to cook when I can get it. It has a mild flavor and firm texture that does not fall apart when cooked. Since the '70s it has been discovered, if you will, by American chefs. Now it can cost as much as swordfish in some places. It is a great alternative to cod, halibut, salmon, striped bass, or swordfish.

1. Heat olive oil in a large heavy-bottomed frying pan over medium heat. Add red and green peppers and sauté for 1 minute.
2. Add garlic and continue to sauté for 1 minute.
3. Reduce heat to low and add green curry paste and coconut milk. Simmer for 3–4 minutes.
4. Add monkfish and continue to simmer for 5 minutes.
5. Salt and pepper to taste. Garnish with cilantro and scallions, served over a bed of rice.

SERVES 4

Pan-Roasted Clams

This impressive but simple-to-prepare dish is great over a bed of rice or pasta.

1. Heat olive oil in a large heavy-bottomed skillet over medium-high heat. Add green peppers and garlic and sauté for 1 minute.
2. Add tomatoes, white wine, clams, and cayenne. Cover and cook for 5–6 minutes or until the clams have opened. Discard any clams that have not opened.
3. Sprinkle with basil and parsley.

SERVES 4

3 tablespoons extra-virgin olive oil

1 medium green pepper, diced

3 garlic cloves, minced

2 medium-to-large tomatoes, seeded and diced

½ cup dry white wine

36 littleneck clams, scrubbed

1 pinch cayenne or red pepper flakes

2 tablespoons chopped fresh basil

2 tablespoons chopped fresh flat-leaf parsley

The Bite

In the early 1980s I decided it was time to branch out, opening a little clam shack called The Bite. It has gone on to be quite well known. Unfortunately, I can't take much of the credit for its success.

At the time I decided to open The Bite, there was really only one option for lunch in Menemsha, a little placed called The Galley. For years The Galley served basic lunch fare, but it also did a lot of fried food—fish-and-chips, clams, shrimp, and scallops. Then they decided to simplify their menu and got rid of their fryers.

Suddenly it was all but impossible to get yourself a fried lunch in Menemsha. It didn't go over well. People started showing up at the back door of the Home Port at midday, looking for a little fried something or other for lunch. It was never my intention to go back into the lunch business. I didn't want to compete with The Galley. There was a gentleman's agreement of sorts in Menemsha that the few restaurants would not directly compete with each other, and I always stuck to that. But there was a demand for fried lunchtime food. The majority of the people coming to the back door during daylight hours were locals. I could not turn them away. Without even knowing it, I was back in the lunch business.

That first year, lunch business was good. But the one thing people seemed to really want, fried clams, I couldn't do. Frying clams is a little tricky. It has always been my policy that if you can't offer customers something cooked the way it should be, don't offer it at all. I'd rather have people disappointed they can't get something than disappointed in what they get. Fried clams have to be made to order. Then they have to be fried twice, once in new oil and then in slightly older oil to brown them up perfectly. At the Home Port, I didn't have two fryers to dedicate to frying clams. I just couldn't do it logistically. Considering I'm a huge fan of fried clams, however, I really wanted to offer them. So if I couldn't do it at the Home Port, I decided to open a place where I could.

Just around the corner from the Home Port's back door was a tiny 14-by-14-foot shingled shack that had housed several little take-out places over the years. Conveniently, it was available, so I leased it, installed a few fryers, mounted a giant shark with working jaws over the front, and called it The Bite.

From the beginning, The Bite was a huge success. I had a couple of kids from my kitchen at the Home Port running it. It was so simple to run, and so close by, all I needed was someone who could fry seafood and count money. One day I ran over to check on things and was kind of hit upside the head by the reality of running two businesses at once. Sam, the kid who was supposed to be working, wasn't there. Someone else was. "Who are you?" I asked the rather insolent young man sitting inside with his feet up on the counter. "Who are you?" he said to me. "I own the place. Where's Sam?" I said. There might have been an expletive or two thrown in there. "Sam had me watch the place while he went down to the beach," the kid said. I was so angry, I thought my head was going to explode. "Well, you tell Sam to come see me when he gets back from the beach," I said.

I went back to the Home Port, fuming. In the time it took me to cover the couple hundred yards between the two places, I decided I would either have to find someone else to run The Bite, which was a problem because I needed all of my best people at the Home Port, or I would sell it. I opted for the latter, already having someone in mind.

Karen Flynn had been a waitress at the Home Port for a few years. One night—half in jest, I think—she said she would buy The Bite from me if I ever wanted to sell it. That very night I took her up on the offer. I made it incredibly easy for her, very much the same way Chet Cummens had done for me with the Home Port. It was the least I could do. One of the many things I learned from Chet was to help out those who had been so good to you over the years.

Karen and her family have done wonderful things with The Bite. Now, when a magazine or TV travel show talks about Menemsha, The Bite is always mentioned right there along with the Home Port. There is always a long line for her famous Bite fries and fried clams. It's become as much of an institution as the Home Port—well, almost.

Fried Clams

1 quart canola oil

4 cups fresh whole clams (soft-shell steamers)

Buttermilk

Dry pancake mix

Making fried clams can be a bit of a messy proposition. Don't be afraid to get your hands dirty, because you will.

1. Heat oil in a heavy-bottomed 4-quart pot to 360°F.
2. Dip clams in buttermilk and drain, then dredge in pancake mix. Make sure each clam is separate and individually coated. Place clams in a strainer and shake off excess pancake mix.
3. Drop clams in oil and fry for 1 minute. Do not overcook.
4. Serve immediately with tartar sauce (page 186) and lemon wedges.

SERVES 4

Stuffed Squid with Tomato Sauce

Buying squid at a fish market can be a little intimidating for those who haven't done it before. Don't worry—most fish markets will clean the squid for you. Make sure it's fresh. The only thing frozen squid should be used for is bait.

1. Remove head and tentacles from squid. Discard head. Remove the innards and rinse squid. Chop tentacles into ¼-inch pieces.
2. Heat olive oil in a nonstick frying pan over medium heat. Add onion and garlic and sauté for 2 minutes.
3. Add chopped tentacles and sauté for 1 minute.
4. Add bread crumbs and sauté for 2 minutes.
5. Remove from heat and place contents of pan in a mixing bowl. Allow to cool.
6. Add parsley, basil, Parmesan cheese, and black olives to the bowl and mix together. Salt and pepper to taste.
7. Stuff the squid bodies with the mixture and secure the opening with a toothpick.
8. Place tomato sauce in a large frying pan over low heat. Add squid to tomato sauce and cook for 10–12 minutes. Be careful not to overcook.
9. Serve over pasta or rice, garnished with parsley and basil.

SERVES 4

8 fresh squid, 5–6 inches long, not counting tentacles

2 tablespoons olive oil

2 tablespoons minced onion

2 garlic cloves, minced

1 cup panko bread crumbs

2 tablespoons chopped fresh flat-leaf parsley

1 tablespoon chopped fresh basil

2 tablespoons grated Parmesan cheese

2 tablespoons chopped black olives

Salt and pepper to taste

4 cups tomato sauce

Calamari

2 quarts canola oil

4 cups squid rings

Buttermilk

Dry pancake mix

As a child, the thought of squid—giant, slimy, boat-crushing monsters from the briny deep—terrified me. In the summer of 1977, I found out how much fun it was to gig for squid at night down on Duter Dock, a summer tradition in Menemsha. As that year was the start of my culinary career, I hardly knew a squid from a jellyfish. After one night of catching, cleaning, and cooking these not-at-all-so-scary sea monsters (they were much smaller than I thought they would be), they became one of my favorite seafoods. The flavor is mild and the texture is tender, not rubbery, when cooked properly.

1. Heat oil in a heavy-bottomed 4-quart pot to 360°F.
2. Dip squid in buttermilk and drain off excess, then dredge in pancake mix. Make sure each piece is separate and individually coated. Place squid in a strainer and shake off excess pancake mix.
3. Drop squid in oil and fry for 1 minute. Do not overcook.
4. Serve immediately with tartar sauce (page 186) and lemon wedges.

SERVES 4

Timing is everything when it comes to frying calamari. The resultant rings should be crispy, golden, and delicious—not overdone.

Fried Soft-Shell Crab

Most—and the best—soft-shell crabs come from the Maryland and Virginia coast. They are harvested as soon as they have molted (grown out of their shells), before they grow their next shells.

When buying soft-shell crabs, be sure to ask the good people at your local fish market to clean them for you. If you find the job left to you, here's what to do: With a pair of sharp kitchen shears, cut off the eye sockets and lower mouth. Then lift up the apron (the shell on the back side) and cut off the gills and apron. It's that simple.

1 tablespoon Old Bay or preferred seafood spice
3 cups flour
3 eggs
½ cup milk
1 sleeve (¼ pound) saltine crackers, finely ground in food processor
2 quarts canola oil
8 soft-shell crabs

1. In a bowl, mix Old Bay and flour.
2. In another bowl, whisk eggs and milk until frothy.
3. Place finely ground saltines in a third bowl.
4. Heat oil to 360°F in a heavy-bottomed 6-quart pot.
5. Dip crabs into flour mixture and shake off excess. Dredge in egg wash and allow excess to drip off. Completely cover crabs with ground crackers, pressing gently.
6. Fry crabs for 2 minutes. Keep them warm in a 200°F oven as frying process continues.
7. Serve immediately with tartar sauce (page 186), cilantro sauce (page 187), dill sauce (page 190), or aioli (page 190).

SERVES 4

Sautéed Soft-Shell Crab

1 tablespoon Old Bay or preferred seafood spice

3 cups flour

8 soft-shell crabs

8 tablespoons butter

8 tablespoons extra-virgin olive oil

3 garlic cloves, thinly sliced

Fresh chopped scallions for garnish

Lemon wedges for garnish

1. Combine Old Bay and flour in a bowl. Dredge each crab in flour mixture.
2. In a large frying pan, heat 2 tablespoons butter and 2 tablespoons olive oil over medium-high heat.
3. Place crabs in pan (as many as will fit without overlapping). Cook for 2 minutes on each side or until golden brown. Repeat cooking process until all crabs are cooked, adding butter and oil as needed.
4. After all the crabs have been cooked, sauté garlic in remaining butter and oil until lightly browned.
5. Cover crabs with garlic and butter-oil mixture and garnish with scallions and lemon wedges. Serve with aioli (page 190) or tartar sauce (page 186).

SERVES 4

For information on cleaning soft-shell crabs, see the Fried Soft-Shell Crab recipe (page 171).

Mussels with Pasta

When I'm in a fish market and I see some very fresh medium-to-large mussels, I often think of this quick and easy dish. The colorful presentation makes it look like you spent hours slaving away in the kitchen. I won't tell if you won't.

1. Prepare pasta, drain, and return to hot pot. Add 2 tablespoons butter and put to the side.
2. In a pot large enough for the mussels with room to spare, heat white wine and reduce by half.
3. Add remaining butter, garlic, peppers, onion, Italian spice, and black pepper. Cook over medium-high heat for 2 minutes.
4. Add mussels and cover pot. Cook for 8–10 minutes or until mussels have opened, occasionally shaking pot.
5. While mussels cook, heat a large serving bowl full of water in the microwave.
6. Reheat pasta in hot water. Dump water and put pasta in serving bowl.
7. When mussels are finished cooking, pour mussels and broth over pasta. Garnish with parsley and scallions, and serve piping hot.

SERVES 4

12 ounces rotini or penne pasta

6 tablespoons butter

2 cups dry white wine

1½ tablespoons minced garlic

2 tablespoons chopped green pepper, cut into ¼-inch pieces

2 tablespoons chopped red pepper, cut into ¼-inch pieces

2 tablespoons chopped yellow pepper, cut into ¼-inch pieces

2 tablespoons chopped onion, cut into ¼-inch pieces

1 tablespoon Italian spices

1 teaspoon black pepper

6 pounds medium to large mussels, scrubbed and debearded

Chopped parsley and scallions for garnish

Seafood Casserole

2 cups rotini (tricolor, spinach, or plain)

5 tablespoons butter

¼ cup minced onion

¼ cup minced celery

1–2 garlic cloves, minced

2 tablespoons flour

1 teaspoon Old Bay or preferred seafood spice

1 cup clam juice

1 cup heavy cream

2 tablespoons dry sherry or extra dry vermouth

1 pound shrimp (20–25 count), peeled and deveined, tails removed

1 pound sea scallops, cut in half

½ pound halibut or monkfish, cut into bite-size pieces

½ pound salmon, cut into bite-size pieces

½ pound lobster meat, cut into bite-size pieces

Salt and pepper to taste

1 cup shredded Monterey Jack cheese

2 cups herb stuffing (page 203)

Chopped flat-leaf parsley for garnish

Chopped chives for garnish

When planning a dinner party, this recipe can be made a day in advance and reheated and served.

1. Preheat oven to 400°F.
2. Boil rotini for 6 minutes and put to the side.
3. Melt 4 tablespoons butter in a saucepan over medium-low heat. Add onion, celery, and garlic and sauté for 2 minutes, stirring constantly.
4. Reduce heat to low. Add flour and cook for 2 minutes, stirring constantly.
5. Add Old Bay, clam juice, heavy cream, and sherry. Cook for 3 minutes over medium-high heat, stirring frequently.

6. Add shrimp, sea scallops, and fish. Cook for 2 minutes, stirring frequently and gently so the fish does not break apart.

7. Butter an ovenproof casserole dish with remaining butter.

8. Pour fish and sauce into casserole dish. Add lobster meat and pasta, and salt and pepper to taste. Sprinkle with cheese and top with herb stuffing.

9. Cook for 20 minutes or until stuffing is golden brown.

10. Garnish with fresh parsley and chives.

SERVES 8–10

Options: Add a little bacon for a contrast in taste. Spice up the sauce with fresh basil, thyme, dill, or parsley. Substitute blanched bite-size potatoes for pasta.

Preparing sauces at home is quick, easy, and tastes much better than store-bought substitutes.

Culinary Components

Lobster Stock	White Sauce
Fish Stock	Lobster Sauce
Shrimp Stock	White Clam Sauce
Clam Broth	Red Clam Sauce
Court Bouillon	Roasted Garlic Sauce
Red Cocktail Sauce	Pesto
Green Cocktail Sauce	Cranberry Mustard Sauce
Tartar Sauce	Mustard Glaze
Mignonette Sauce	Ginger Glaze
Cilantro Sauce	Thai Glaze
Dill Sauce	Casino Butter
Aioli	Seafood Butter Sauce
Ginger Saffron Sauce	Herb Stuffing

Culinary Components

STOCKS AND BROTHS

Friends and neighbors rarely turn down my dinner invitations. What can I say? They like the way I cook. Many show up early and help in the preparation, hoping to pick up a trick or two along the way. And what people find most interesting are the simmering pots of stock and broths I inevitably have on the stove.

The reason restaurant food is considered better tasting and fancier than mom's regular fare is primarily because professionals use stocks. Now that the Food Network and other cooking shows have made us all foodies and expert cooks, mom can cook like a pro. Still, many aspiring home chefs shy away from the "stock pot." Those words conjure up a vision of a huge pot filled with meat bones, vegetables, eggshells, herbs, and who knows

what else simmering for hours on end. And I'm not going to lie: It does take some time to make a good stock, and they can be a little messy. But they're oh-so-worth-it.

Preparing stocks is not really that difficult. Once you have made a stock or two and tasted the difference they make in your cooking, I think you will agree that stocks are well worth the time and effort. Your homemade soups and sauces will have a much richer flavor, and your friends will be calling you "chef." It's that simple.

Lobster Stock

Check out your local fish market for any lobster bodies they might have. They are cheap, and otherwise unsalable. They are not always available, so have your fish merchant let you know when they have some. They keep great in the freezer until it is time to make the stock.

1. Preheat oven to 400°F.
2. Rinse lobster bodies and chop with a cleaver or heavy knife.
3. Place lobster bodies, onions, celery, and carrots on a baking sheet. Spray with vegetable oil.
4. Bake for 6 minutes. Do not allow to burn.
5. Remove from oven and place in a 6- to 8-quart heavy pot. Add parsley, thyme, bay leaves, and water.
6. Bring almost to a boil. Reduce heat and simmer for 30 minutes.
7. Strain and cool. Remember, do not cover anything in the refrigerator until it has completely cooled. Stock will last 3–4 days in the refrigerator or 6 months the in freezer. Salt and white pepper can be added to taste.

MAKES 2 QUARTS

4 pounds lobster bodies

1 medium onion, coarsely chopped

4 stalks celery, coarsely chopped

2 carrots, coarsely chopped

Vegetable oil spray

4 parsley sprigs

2 thyme sprigs

2 bay leaves

2 quarts water

Want that great restaurant taste in your next meal? Use homemade stock.

Fish Stock

3–4 pounds fish bones, no gills

1 medium onion, coarsely chopped

4 stalks celery, coarsely chopped

2 carrots, coarsely chopped

Vegetable oil spray

4 parsley sprigs

2 thyme sprigs

2 bay leaves

2 quarts water

Start with a trip to the fish market for fish bones (often called racks). You want racks from mild whitefish like flounder, haddock, cod, striped bass, or grouper. More often than not, you will get them at little or no cost. The gills will have to be removed. Use heavy-duty kitchen shears to do this. Better yet, tip your local fishmonger, and they might just do it for you.

I use my fish stock from the freezer to poach salmon and other fish. After removing the fish, strain the stock and refreeze until needed again.

1. Preheat oven to 400°F.
2. Rinse bones and chop with a cleaver or heavy knife.
3. Place bones, onions, celery, and carrots on a sheet pan. Spray with vegetable oil.
4. Bake at 400°F for 6 minutes. Do not allow to burn.
5. Remove from oven and place in a 6- to 8-quart heavy pot. Add parsley, thyme, bay leaves, and water.
6. Bring almost to a boil. Reduce heat and simmer for 30 minutes.
7. Strain and cool. Remember, do not cover anything in the refrigerator until it has completely cooled. Stock will last 3–4 days in refrigerator or 6 months in freezer. Salt and white pepper can be used to taste.

MAKES 2 QUARTS

The Kennedys

Almost without exception, whenever a newspaper or magazine or television travel show does a piece on the Home Port, they say the same thing: "It's where you'll see a local fisherman eating next to a Kennedy."

Well, it's true.

I will never forget my first encounter with a member of that famous family. It was one of the first years I owned the Home Port. I had to go out to the front desk for something, I don't remember what exactly. Standing with her back turned to the hostess podium was this elegantly dressed woman looking out the window. I asked the hostess whatever I had gone out there to inquire, but she didn't seem much interested in answering my question. Her attention was firmly placed on the woman looking out the window. When the woman turned and I saw who it was, I have to say I was more than a little taken aback. It was Jackie Kennedy Onassis, who very politely asked the hostess how long it would be before they would be seated.

We saw quite a bit of Jackie before the death of her second husband, and in the years that followed with Maurice Tempelsman. By then, Jackie had resumed spending large portions of her summers on the Island. Maurice was an avid boater, and often they would tie up his yacht at the dock and come in for dinner straight off the boat. Sometimes John Jr. or Caroline or other members of the family would join them, but usually it was just the two of them. No security—just a happy couple out for dinner. We were very protective of them. As with all of our celebrity customers, we made sure they weren't bothered while they were at the Home Port. I think it's one reason so many famous people ate there. They could sit next to a local fisherman or a vacationing family from New Jersey and not have to worry about being bothered. Of course, the fisherman or the family from New Jersey didn't have our staff watching, waiting, to intercept anyone who forgot that celebrity customers were not to be approached. Sadly, we didn't see much of Jackie in the few years before her death. Word would get out that she was on the Island, but she kept to herself.

We saw a lot of Patrick Kennedy over the years, too. More often than not he would come in alone, off his boat, and have a quiet dinner. He was always very nice to everyone.

But I would have to say our most frequent customer from the famous family was John Jr. It wasn't uncommon for him to ride his bike up in the afternoon, much to the delight of our female employees, and come to the back door and make a reservation for that night. Over the years we saw his much-publicized romances unfold in the Home Port dining room. It was always entertaining to see who he would bring with him—Ashley Richardson, Sarah Jessica

Parker, and Daryl Hannah being the more notable of the many girlfriends he brought in for dinner. We knew who he was dating and when they had broken up before any of the tabloids did.

My sister, who worked for years as my hostess, tells the story best about a dining room row between John Jr. and Daryl Hannah. She had a front-row seat for the whole thing. As she tells it, John had come in earlier in the day to make a reservation for two. He had been dating Daryl for a while by then, and they came in once or twice a week. But that night he showed up for his reservation alone. He picked an old *National Geographic* out of the stack we kept by the door for people to read while they wait. When his table was ready, he went and sat down, alone, and ordered dinner. He was very nice to everyone, as always. Everyone knew something was up. No one could remember seeing him eat alone before. He sat and ate and read the magazine. Then Daryl came in and asked my sister if John was there. "Yes, dear," my sister replied. "He's at your usual table."

Daryl went over and sat down. John hardly looked up. The waitress came and asked Daryl if she wanted anything to eat. "I'm not hungry," she replied. John went right on eating his dinner, flipping through the magazine while Daryl just sat and watched him. When he finished he got up, paid, and went out. A few weeks later it was all over the news that they had split up.

News of John's untimely death sent shockwaves across the Island. He was on his way to the Vineyard when the plane he was piloting went down only a few miles out. Navy and coast guard ships dotted the horizon as they searched for the wreckage. And I watched as his uncle, Teddy Kennedy, arrived at the coast guard station that overlooks Menemsha—only a few hundred yards from the restaurant—and somberly boarded a helicopter to go out and identify his nephew's body. John's ashes, along with those of his new bride and her sister, were sprinkled in the waters off the Island. I can't help but wonder what he might have become. He will be missed.

Shrimp Stock

Whenever I peel shrimp to prepare a recipe, I save the shells and put them in the freezer until I have a large bag full. Then I simply put them in enough water to partially cover them and add a bay leaf. Bring the water to a boil, then reduce the heat and simmer for 8 to 10 minutes. Strain off the shells and freeze the stock until the next time you prepare a shrimp recipe.

I cook a lot of shrimp at home for shrimp cocktail and shrimp salad. I use shrimp stock from the freezer whenever I boil shrimp. Each time it is used it becomes more fortified with that wonderful shrimp flavor. If you don't boil enough shrimp to start a base, fear not: Shrimp base can be found at most upscale grocery stores and online.

Clam Broth

I always save any remaining broth after steaming clams and put it in the freezer for when recipes call for it. Be sure to check the salt content because it can become a little concentrated if reused more than once. Clam broth is usually available at fish markets and in small bottles at most supermarkets. Clam base can also be found online.

Court Bouillon

2 quarts water

16 ounces clam juice

1 small onion, chopped

4–5 celery stalks, chopped

4–5 bay leaves

4–5 cloves

1 teaspoon Old Bay or preferred
    seafood spice

1 lemon, quartered

2 parsley sprigs

2 thyme sprigs

This easy-to-make bouillon adds flavor to poached fish and boiled shellfish. The best part is you can use it over and over, and it gets more flavorful with each use. Simply put it in the freezer until the next time.

1. Place all ingredients in a 4- to 6-quart heavy-bottomed pot. Bring to a boil.
2. Reduce heat and simmer for 15 minutes. Strain.
3. Court bouillon can be used immediately or when cooled. When frozen, defrost at room temperature. Good for up to 6 months or 20 uses.

MAKES 2½ QUARTS

Options: Use white wine, sherry, or cider vinegar along with listed ingredients, depending on taste. Thyme, parsley, cilantro, and other favorite herbs and spices can also be used. Experiment and find what suits you best.

There is nothing like the smell of simmering stock.

Sauces, Glazes, and Stuffing

Red Cocktail Sauce

Red cocktail sauce is a seafood essential, but please, please, please do yourself and anyone you are cooking for a favor and make your own.

We've been using this classic recipe for the requisite seafood restaurant condiment since the 1950s. Handed down from Chet Cummens, this semi-hot sauce livens up nearly every kind of seafood, but in my opinion, is best on cold seafood items. Any seafood restaurant worth going to makes their cocktail sauce on the premises. The Home Port would go through four to five gallons of it a day—that's a lot of cocktail sauce. Of course, there are more premade cocktail sauces than anyone can count—and none of them are worth a damn.

Cocktail sauce is simple to make and keeps well in the refrigerator. Experiment. Find the combination of ingredients you like best. More contemporary versions include chopped onion, garlic, cilantro, and all kinds of chili peppers.

½ cup ketchup

¼ cup chili sauce

3 tablespoons grated horseradish

1 tablespoon lemon or lime juice

1 teaspoon Worcestershire sauce

½ teaspoon Tabasco

1. Mix all the ingredients in a large bowl until blended thoroughly.
2. Refrigerate for at least 2 hours before serving.

MAKES 1 CUP

Red cocktail sauce pairs nicely with hot and cold seafood, including succulent clam fritters.

Green Cocktail Sauce

1 cup salsa verde, medium heat

½ avocado

¼ cup horseradish

½ cup cilantro leaves

1 teaspoon salt

1 teaspoon white pepper

1 tablespoon Worcestershire
  sauce

1 tablespoon green Tabasco

Juice of 1 lemon

This green sauce can be used as a substitute for red sauce, but I prefer to serve both. The flavor is pungent and zippy, which complements cold seafood and raw shellfish.

1. Put ½ cup salsa and all the other ingredients in a food processor. Blend for 20 seconds.
2. Place in a bowl and add remaining salsa.
3. Chill for at least 1 hour before serving.

MAKES 2 CUPS

Tartar Sauce

1 cup mayonnaise

½ cup chopped dill pickles

2 tablespoons minced onion

1 tablespoon chopped fresh
  parsley

1 tablespoon capers

Salt and white pepper to taste

You can't have fried seafood without tartar sauce. I've had a lot of tartar sauce over the years, but you aren't going to find any much better than this recipe. And please, please, please, whatever you do, take the 10 minutes it takes to make it yourself. The store-bought stuff just isn't as good.

1. Place all the ingredients in a large bowl and mix thoroughly.
2. Refrigerate for at least 2 hours before serving.

MAKES 2 CUPS

Options: Add Dijon mustard, green olives, tarragon, cilantro, lemon zest, or Tabasco for a new twist on an old favorite.

Mignonette Sauce

This is a tasty alternative to the traditional red cocktail sauce.

1. Mix all ingredients in a bowl.
2. Refrigerate for a half hour before using.

MAKES ½ CUP

Options: Try adding any of the following: fresh chopped basil, tarragon, or cilantro. Substitute rice vinegar, raspberry vinegar, or sherry vinegar for a subtle change of flavor. Or add wasabi and chopped pickled ginger, fresh garlic, or lemon, lime, orange, or grapefruit juice. For a little more zip, seed and dice 2 to 3 jalapeños and add to the base sauce.

1 tablespoon minced garlic

2 tablespoons finely chopped shallots

1 tablespoon finely chopped fresh parsley

¼ cup red wine vinegar

½ teaspoon salt

2 teaspoons fresh cracked black pepper

Cilantro Sauce

Try this as a dipping sauce for fried seafood as an alternative to tartar sauce.

1. Place cilantro, garlic, orange juice, orange zest, tomato paste, and cumin in food processor and pulse until fully incorporated but not pureed.
2. Add honey and olive oil while pulsing. Do not fully puree.
3. Refrigerate for 1 hour before serving.

MAKES 1 CUP

2 cups fresh cilantro leaves

1 tablespoon minced fresh garlic

2 tablespoons orange juice

1 tablespoon orange zest

2 tablespoons tomato paste

1 teaspoon ground cumin

1 tablespoon honey

¼ cup extra-virgin olive oil

Third Time's a Charm

It doesn't matter who you are, getting a table at the Home Port without a reservation is not an easy thing to do. People would sometimes make reservations a year in advance. Usually, the wait for a table was at least a couple weeks. Of course, every night there were a handful of people who would roll the dice, come in without a reservation, and pray someone would not show up for their reservation. We always did the best we could to fit people in, but when you're booked solid, you're booked solid. People would come when the restaurant opened and put their names down and wait patiently, more or less, until something opened up. We usually got them in, but it took a while.

Now, after all that, I hate to say it, but there was somewhat of a double standard when it came to celebrities. They really are different than you and me, and not just because they have money. Celebrities are part of what made the Home Port such a wonderful place. I'll be the first to say that. So, of course, we always did our best to accommodate them to a certain point. It was our policy to never bump anyone—that is just bad business—but we could be very creative seating people when we had to be.

One incredibly busy night there was one such celebrity who came in looking for a table. He wanted to sit and eat with his family and was politely informed by my sister, Judy, who had no idea who he was, that we would not be able to accommodate him that night, but if he would like to make a future reservation, she would be more than happy to do that for him. He declined the offer and bid her goodnight. The next night he came back and was told the same thing. And the next night. He was always very gracious about it. He didn't get angry or use the old go-to so many celebrities use: "Don't you know who I am?"

As he was walking out, Madeline, my wife, asked my oblivious sister why Bruce Willis was leaving. Judy explained that this was the third night in a row he had come in looking for a table. "Do you know who that is?" Madeline asked.

Word of what had just happened got back to the kitchen fast. I went out the back door and saw someone I thought might be him walking through the parking lot. I called out his name and ran to catch up with him. Bruce looked at me warily, probably thinking I was some flunky out of the kitchen wanting an autograph. I explained to him who I was, and that I understood he had been in a couple nights already and been unable to get a table. He was really very nice about it. I promised him if he came back in an hour, we would have a table for him. "You don't have to do that," he said, to which I replied, "Getting a table here is like *Die Hard*." He thought that was very funny. Of course, when I went back and relayed to everyone in the kitchen what I said, thinking I had been very clever, my son, Michael, rolled his eyes at me and shook his head. "That's the cheesiest thing I think I have ever heard you say," he said. Nothing like your teenage children to keep you humble.

Bruce showed up at the appointed time. He had his children with him. We gave him a wonderful table that overlooked the patio. When it came time to order, he asked to see me. I went out right away. He seemed very glad to see me again. "Do you have any egg noodles? My daughter only eats egg noodles," he said. I explained I could make her just about anything, but we didn't have any egg noodles. "It has to be Pennsylvania Dutch egg noodles," he said. Now, I've had some unusual requests over the years, and this ranked right there at the top of them. Most of the time we can figure something out, but this was not one of those times. I felt bad telling him. He just shrugged and got up and went across the street to the market, where he obviously knew they had exactly what he wanted. He came back with a package of the noodles and brought them back into the kitchen for me. We made them up and everyone seemed as happy as clams—pardon the pun.

It's funny how people react to different celebrities. Tom Hanks can walk up to the back door, get his dinner, and sit down on the patio and eat, and not a single person will bother him. Usually, it isn't a problem. There is an understanding most people on the Island, and certainly our customers, have about bothering the many celebrities that come in. You don't. But you put Bruce Willis in the dining room, and people are literally climbing on top of each other to gawk at him. The first night, we made the mistake of putting him right by a window. People were lined up, looking in and banging on the window. Madeline had to go out and shoo them away. Thankfully, he was accustomed to such behavior. He would give them a smile and a wave and then go back to his dinner.

We saw a lot of Bruce Willis and his family that year. It kept us very busy, but we were always happy to have him. And we always had egg noodles on hand after that.

Dill Sauce

1 cup sour cream

1 cup mayonnaise

¼ cup horseradish

⅓ cup chopped fresh dill

2–3 tablespoons milk or half-
and-half

Salt and white pepper to taste

*This Home Port favorite is usually served with fried zucchini but is fantastic
with cold seafood and vegetables. I love it with shrimp!*

1. Place sour cream, mayonnaise, horseradish, and dill in a bowl
   and mix thoroughly.
2. Add enough milk to thin sauce as necessary. Sauce should pour
   easily.
3. Add salt and pepper to taste.

MAKES 2½ CUPS

Aioli

4 cloves garlic

2 tablespoons lemon juice

1½ teaspoons Dijon mustard

½ teaspoon salt

⅛ teaspoon white pepper

3 egg yolks at room
temperature

1½ cups extra-virgin olive oil

*Purists still make this useful sauce whisking it by hand. I say if you have a food
processor, use it. Be sure the egg yolks are at room temperature to ensure the
proper consistency.*

1. Put all the ingredients except olive oil in a food processor and
   blend for 15 seconds.
2. Slowly add olive oil and continue blending. The sauce should
   have the consistency of mayonnaise.
3. Refrigerate at least 2 hours before using.

MAKES 2 CUPS

Option: Add zest of lemon for more tang.

Ginger Saffron Sauce

This sauce is ideal for topping any seafood. I often add crabmeat at the end of the sauce's preparation for that little something extra.

1. In a heavy-bottomed saucepan, heat ginger, saffron, bay leaf, stock, and wine to a gentle boil. Reduce by half.
2. Add heavy cream and reduce by half.
3. In a separate saucepan, melt butter. Add flour and cook over low heat for 3 minute, stirring frequently.
4. Add sauce to roux (butter and flour mixture) and stir until thick and creamy.
5. Strain sauce. Add salt and pepper to taste. Can be served either hot or cold.

MAKES 2 CUPS

⅓ cup peeled and chopped fresh ginger, cut into ¼-inch pieces
½ teaspoon saffron
1 bay leaf
2 cups fish or chicken stock
½ cup Riesling
2 cups heavy cream
1 tablespoon butter
1 tablespoon flour
Salt and white pepper to taste

White Sauce

This sauce serves as the base for a number of different sauces. Add cheese, and you have a wonderful cheese sauce. Add fish stock, and you have sauce for a seafood preparation. White sauce is easy to make and ready to take on any flavor profile you wish.

1. Melt butter in a saucepan over medium-low heat. Add flour and stir constantly with a wire whisk until sauce is smooth and thick, about 3 minutes.
2. Add cream. Continue to stir.
3. Remove from heat. Add nutmeg and salt and pepper to taste.

MAKES 3 CUPS

Option: Add 2 bay leaves, 1 chicken bouillon cube, and a couple dashes of Tabasco and Worcestershire sauce.

¼ cup butter
¼ cup flour
3 cups heavy cream or half-and-half
Fresh grated or ground nutmeg to taste
Salt and white pepper to taste

Lobster Sauce

4 tablespoons butter

4 ounces lobster meat, chopped

1 tablespoon lobster base

2 tablespoons flour

1 teaspoon paprika

1 tablespoon minced shallots

2 tablespoons dry sherry

1 cup heavy cream

2 egg yolks

2 drops Tabasco

4 drops Worcestershire sauce

Salt and white pepper

Who wouldn't like this sauce to top off any seafood dish?

1. Melt butter in a large nonstick frying pan over medium heat. Add lobster meat and cook for 1 minute.
2. Remove lobster meat and put to the side.
3. Add lobster base, flour, paprika, shallots, and sherry and cook for 2 minutes on medium heat.
4. In a bowl, combine heavy cream and egg yolks and beat until smooth.
5. Add cream and egg mixture to frying pan along with Tabasco and Worcestershire sauce and wait for sauce to thicken.
6. Add the lobster meat, stir, and remove from heat.
7. Salt and pepper to taste.

MAKES 2 CUPS

Fresh lobster plays the starring role in rich lobster sauce—perfect with just about any seafood entrée.

White Clam Sauce

When making this sauce, chopped fresh sea clams are preferred, though other varieties will also do. When buying clams for this sauce or the red clam sauce, be sure to give your fish market a couple days' notice, because they may not regularly stock fresh sea clams. Frozen will work, but be sure to completely thaw and drain them.

I like to serve this sauce over fresh fettuccini or linguine. Fresh steamed littlenecks placed on top or on the side of the pasta add that certain little something to the presentation.

1. Heat olive oil in a heavy-bottomed pot over medium-low heat. Cook garlic for 2 minutes. Do not brown.
2. Add flour and stir with a wire whisk for 3 minutes.
3. Add clam juice, heavy cream, and bay leaf and continue to stir.
4. Warm clams in a separate saucepan.
5. Add clams to sauce and heat thoroughly. Add pepper to taste.
6. After pouring over pasta, garnish with basil and parsley.

MAKES 6 CUPS

¼ cup extra-virgin olive oil

1 tablespoon minced fresh garlic

3 tablespoons flour

2 cups clam juice

1 cup heavy cream

1 bay leaf

1½ pints chopped fresh sea clams

Fresh ground black pepper to taste

Chopped fresh basil for garnish

Chopped fresh parsley for garnish

Red Clam Sauce

¼ cup extra-virgin olive oil

2 tablespoons chopped fresh garlic

2 cups chopped onion, cut into ¼-inch pieces

1½ cups chopped green bell pepper, cut into ¼-inch pieces

1 cup celery, chopped into ¼-inch pieces

½ teaspoon crushed red pepper flakes

2 tablespoons Italian spice

3 bay leaves

3 cups diced tomatoes

3 cups marinara sauce

½ cup red wine (optional)

3 pints sea clams, chopped and drained

¼ cup chopped fresh parsley for garnish

Traditionally this sauce is served over linguine, but any pasta works just as well. Whenever possible, try to use fresh pasta. To add to the presentation, steam a few littleneck clams to go on top or on the side of the dish.

1. Heat olive oil in a heavy-bottomed pot over medium heat. Add garlic, onions, green peppers, celery, and red pepper flakes and cook for 4 minutes, stirring occasionally.

2. Add Italian spice, bay leaves, tomatoes, marinara, and red wine. Simmer for 45 minutes, stirring occasionally.

3. Add clams and continue to cook for 4 minutes.

4. Pour over pasta and garnish with fresh chopped parsley.

MAKES 2 QUARTS

Roasted Garlic Sauce

This is a great dip for seafood or veggies. I always keep some roasted garlic in my refrigerator when I want a milder garlic taste in dishes that call for fresh garlic.

1. Preheat oven to 400°F.
2. Sprinkle olive oil over an ovenproof dish.
3. Break open garlic cloves and spread out in a single layer on dish. Bake for 25 minutes.
4. Remove from oven and allow garlic to cool.
5. Peel garlic cloves and place them on a cutting board with a pinch of salt. Mash cloves with a fork.
6. Combine mashed garlic with mayonnaise, sour cream, and Old Bay and mix thoroughly. Salt and pepper to taste.
7. Chill for 1 hour before serving.

MAKES 1 CUP

Options: Add any of your favorite herbs or spices.

1 tablespoon extra-virgin olive oil

2 garlic bulbs (heads)

½ cup mayonnaise

½ cup sour cream

1 teaspoon Old Bay or preferred seafood spice

Salt and pepper to taste

Pesto

2 cups fresh basil leaves
½ cup grated Parmesan cheese
½ cup pine nuts
4 garlic cloves
½ cup extra-virgin olive oil

Pesto is excellent on grilled or broiled fish and seafood. It goes well with everything, really—pasta, salads, vegetables, chicken, and even on toasted crusty bread.

Be sure to always use fresh basil for your pesto. The difference is noticeable. Pesto stores well in the refrigerator for up to 2 weeks and is good for several months when frozen.

1. Combine basil, Parmesan cheese, pine nuts, and garlic in a food processor and chop.
2. Slowly add olive oil while pulsing.
3. Be sure not to overprocess. Pesto should be well blended but not pureed.

MAKES 2 CUPS

Options: Walnuts, almonds, or hazelnuts can be substituted for pine nuts.

A Trump through the Tall Grass

As luck would have it, I was in the office doing some administrative work one afternoon when the phone rang. It was a woman with a sultry, gravelly voice hoping for a reservation that night at 7:30 for ten people. "I'm sorry, we're booked solid for the next week," I said. She hung up even before I could get it all out. A minute later the phone rang again. I recognized her voice immediately. "The reservation is for Donald Trump," she said.

It was widely known Trump was on the Island when she called. His yacht, which was more the size of a navy destroyer than a pleasure boat, was anchored just offshore—it was too big to get into the harbor—and had been there for a couple days already. We had been hearing stories since his arrival about how lavish this thing was, with solid gold door latches and other subtle reminders of his wealth. Rumor had it that Donald was out there with Ivana, his wife at the time, their children, and her parents.

I put the woman on hold and looked at the reservation book a little more closely. I can't remember who it was that had a reservation, but Donald Trump would not have been the most famous (or wealthy) person in the dining room that night. Not even close. And that person had made a reservation. "I'd like to help you out, but I can't bump someone else. I'm sorry. I'd be happy to book you next week," I said. "No," she replied rather sharply. "That just won't do."

A couple minutes later she called back, insisting on a table. "I'm sorry, we're booked," I said. "I can recommend someplace else if you'd like. There are many very good restaurants on the Island. I'm sure Mr. Trump would have an enjoyable dinner at any of them." "No," she snapped and hung up the phone.

I hadn't even put the phone down when it rang again. This conversation made the previous ones seem like pleasant exchanges between good friends. It bordered on threatening. I mean, really, it's a dinner reservation. I'm sure the chef on the boat could boil a lobster. She called back again, with another veiled threat. Now, over the years I've been threatened a time or two by self-important people. But this was a little more than some big-shot lawyer from Long Island who couldn't get a table by a window or whose jumbo lobster wasn't quite jumbo enough (they never are for people like that). But after all, it is my job, my life's work as a restaurateur, to make people happy. And if dinner in my restaurant on that particular night would make Donald Trump happy, then it was my job to see to that. "Fine," I told her after the fifth or sixth call.

Around four o'clock that afternoon, six or seven burly guys in white sailor outfits came in the restaurant. They were very serious-looking dudes, but in their little white outfits, there was something comical about them. They came through and did a security sweep of the place. Having served former presidents and billionaires and the like, having armed security personnel go through the place was something I had become accustomed to, though I'm never quite sure what they are looking for exactly, and sometimes I wonder if they are either.

Seven-thirty rolled around, and in came the guys in their little white outfits followed by Ivana, her children, and her parents and a few other people. No Donald. I guess he didn't want to eat at my restaurant that badly after all. They were shown to their table, and the security guys took their posts on the patio. Now, I had seen Ivana Trump on television, but I have to admit, the TV didn't do her justice. She was a stunningly beautiful woman. She wore an all-white dress and these ridiculously tall heels. *Wow* is about all I have to say about that. They had their dinner without incident, then everyone but Ivana got up and went out the front door to wait for her on the patio. And waited. And waited. The next thing I knew, the security guys were buzzing all around looking for her. She was gone.

Someone then said he saw her go out the back door of the dining room. That was an emergency exit, and there were only two places you could go out that door: down to the water and then around the front of the building, or around the back. To go around the back of the restaurant from there, you start by going through the massive, thorny privacy hedges that block the back of the restaurant. I know firsthand that getting through those hedges is not a pleasant experience. Once through the hedges, you have to scale a short fence and cross a small yard with tall wild grass where we let our two Labs run, so you can imagine what that was like. After scaling the fence (or using the gate, if you knew it was there), you have to go around a small pond tightly guarded by a rather vicious flock of ducks—we called them our guard ducks—and after getting through all of that, you have to go back down where we kept the trash cans—which can be less than pleasant late in the evening, when it's still warm out and they are quickly filling up with garbage from the kitchen and dining room—with an equally vicious flock of seagulls circling overhead. All of this is well away from the restaurant, of course, and well out of view. It was quite a hike.

Finally, we saw Ivana pop into the parking lot from around the back of the restaurant, looking more than a little worse for wear, holding her heels in one hand, yelling at her family in whatever language it was she spoke. The security guys went running after her with everyone else in their wake.

"Why didn't she just use the front door like everyone else?" one of the waitresses asked me as we watched the whole thing from the front door. "Probably because everyone else does," I said. "What good is having all that money if you do things the same as everyone else?"

Cranberry Mustard Sauce

Cranberries are not just for Thanksgiving! This sauce is especially good on grilled shrimp but also goes well with poultry.

1. Combine all the ingredients in a heavy-bottomed saucepan.
2. Over medium heat, whisk for approximately 3 minutes or until smooth.

MAKES 2 CUPS

1 16-ounce can jellied cranberry sauce

2 tablespoons stone-ground mustard

1½ tablespoons light brown sugar

1 teaspoon grated fresh ginger

2 teaspoons lemon juice

Mustard Glaze

Brush this great glaze on seafood during cooking, or use as a marinade or for dipping.

Whisk all the ingredients together in a bowl. Refrigerate until use.

MAKES 1 CUP

¾ cup mayonnaise

⅓ cup stone-ground mustard

1 tablespoon chopped fresh dill

1 teaspoon light brown sugar

1 teaspoon lemon juice

3–4 drops Worcestershire sauce

Salt and pepper to taste

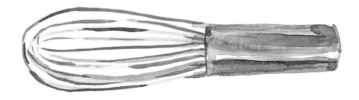

Ginger Glaze

½ cup mayonnaise

1 tablespoon peeled and grated fresh ginger

1 tablespoon soy sauce

1 tablespoon stone-ground mustard

1 tablespoon honey

¼ cup pineapple juice

¼ teaspoon Worcestershire sauce

1 tablespoon chopped fresh dill

Fresh ground black pepper to taste

Use this glaze for marinating, dipping, or basting seafood.

Whisk all the ingredients together in a bowl. Refrigerate until use.

MAKES 1 CUP

Thai Glaze

½ cup mayonnaise

3 tablespoons sesame oil

3 tablespoons soy sauce

1 tablespoon raspberry vinegar

2 tablespoons light brown sugar

1½ teaspoons peeled and grated fresh ginger

1 tablespoon chopped fresh basil

1 tablespoon chopped fresh garlic

1 tablespoon minced shallots

1½ teaspoons green Thai curry paste

Fresh ground black pepper to taste

Another great glaze for marinating, dipping, or basting seafood.

Whisk all the ingredients together in a bowl. Refrigerate until use.

MAKES 1 CUP

Casino Butter

There is an old saying about casino butter: It can make an old shoe taste good. And it's true. I've been using this recipe for years—and will for years to come.

1. Mix all the ingredients well in a bowl.
2. Refrigerate until use.

MAKES 2 CUPS

1 pound butter, softened

8 slices bacon, cooked and chopped

2 tablespoons finely chopped green bell pepper

2 tablespoons finely chopped onion

2 tablespoons finely chopped parsley

2 tablespoons minced fresh garlic

2 tablespoons lemon juice

3–4 dashes Tabasco

3–4 dashes Worcestershire sauce

Savory casino butter takes clams to a whole new culinary level.

Seafood Butter Sauce

⅓ cup minced shallots

½ cup dry white wine

2 cups fish stock

1 bay leaf

4 tablespoons butter

1 teaspoon Dijon mustard

1 tablespoon chopped fresh chives

1 teaspoon lemon zest

Salt and pepper to taste

A wonderful finishing sauce for broiled seafood.

1. Heat shallots and wine in a saucepan over medium-low heat until wine is nearly evaporated.
2. Add fish stock and bay leaf. Reduce by half.
3. Remove from heat and discard bay leaf. Add butter 1 tablespoon at a time while whisking gently.
4. Add mustard, chives, and lemon zest and whisk gently. Add salt and pepper to taste and serve immediately.

MAKES 1½ CUPS

Herb Stuffing

This stuffing was used primarily for the baked-stuffed scallops at the Home Port, but it also goes great on any baked or broiled fish and is excellent for casseroles. It can also be frozen and used when needed.

Combine all the ingredients in a large bowl. Add enough melted butter to moisten the stuffing sufficiently.

MAKES 4 CUPS

¼ pound Ritz crackers, broken into approximately ¼-inch pieces

¼ pound panko bread crumbs

1 tablespoon coarsely chopped fresh parsley

½ teaspoon black pepper

½ teaspoon salt

2 teaspoons minced fresh garlic

1 tablespoon coarsely chopped fresh dill

⅓ cup grated Parmesan cheese

1 teaspoon paprika

8–12 tablespoons butter, melted

So simple and easy to prepare, herb stuffing complements just about any broiled seafood.

Key lime pie (page 207)

Desserts

Traditional Piecrust

Graham Cracker Piecrust

Key Lime Pie

Blueberry Pie

Peanut Butter Pie

Pecan Pie

Chocolate Mint Pie

Nantucket Cranberry Pie

Chocolate Bread Pudding

Chet's Pecan Rolls

Desserts

There are a lot of people—my wife included—who consider dessert the best part of the meal. At the Home Port, dessert was included in the price of the meal. After key lime pie, pecan and blueberry ran close behind in popularity, though they were all pretty darn good.

PIECRUSTS

Traditional Piecrust

5 cups pastry or all-purpose flour

1 teaspoon salt

12 tablespoons chilled butter (1½ sticks), cut into ¼- to ½-inch pieces

1½ cups chilled vegetable shortening

1 cup ice-cold water

This can get messy the first couple times you try it. Many people also find preparing their own piecrust somewhat intimidating—or too time consuming—and go out and get the store-bought stuff. Though store-bought piecrusts can be good, I encourage you to roll up your sleeves and dive in. Once you do, you'll never want store-bought crust again.

This recipe will make 4 open-face pies or 2 covered pies. If you have left-over dough, it will keep in the freezer for about a month.

1. Place flour, salt, butter, and shortening in a large mixer bowl. Mix for 1 minute on low speed.
2. Increase speed of mixer to medium and continue mixing for 30 seconds.
3. Reduce mixing speed to low and slowly add cold water. Mix for 30 seconds.
4. Increase mixer speed to medium for 30 seconds or until dough forms in two firm balls.
5. Chill for 20–30 minutes before rolling.

MAKES 4 9- TO 10-INCH PIECRUSTS

Graham Cracker Piecrust

This is an easy substitute for traditional piecrust and works particularly well with refrigerated pies.

1. Mix ingredients and place in a pie plate. Spread evenly on the bottom and sides of the pie plate.
2. Place a second pie plate (clean and dry) on top of the mixture. Add pressure and hold for 30 seconds and remove. It's that simple.

MAKES 1 10-INCH PIECRUST

1½ cups graham cracker crumbs
¼ cup sugar
5 tablespoons butter, melted

PIES AND SWEETS

Key Lime Pie

Ever since Chet Cummens added key lime pie to the dessert menu in the late '60s, it has been the most popular dessert at the Home Port. Both tart and sweet, it's wonderfully refreshing. Top it with a dollop of whipped cream, and you're all set.

1. Combine egg yolks, lime juice, lime zest, and optional food coloring in a glass mixing bowl. Whisk until color is consistent.
2. Add condensed milk and whisk until color is consistent.
3. Pour filling into piecrust. Chill for 4 hours before serving.
4. Top with whipped cream or nondairy whipped topping.

MAKES 1 PIE

5 egg yolks or ⅓ cup pasteurized egg yolks
¾ cup fresh-squeezed lime juice (or from concentrate)
Zest of 1 lime
1–2 drops green food coloring (optional)
2¾ cups (2 14-ounce cans) condensed milk
1 10-inch graham cracker piecrust (above)

When the Teacher Becomes the Student

Key lime pie has been the Home Port's most popular dessert since Chet Cummens introduced it in the late '60s. It's been lauded in the *New York Times* and *Boston Globe* and a handful of television travel shows. Some people like it because of the tartness; others like it because it is sweet. Actually, it's a combination of both. And, yes, it does have a calorie or two in it. Chet always used to tell people who fretted about calories to eat their dessert in the dark. "Calories don't count in the dark," he would say. He had another piece of advice for those who insisted on seeing what they were eating: "Use a small fork. You don't get as many calories that way." I have to admit I have borrowed both of those lines over the years.

For nearly twenty years I used Chet's recipe, but a lovely, sweet little old lady convinced me to change it. As one of my greatest pleasures is sharing what I know about cooking, I would host cooking demonstrations at the Home Port for the Island's seniors. They would come in the morning and we would take over the kitchen, swapping cooking secrets and enjoying our creations afterwards. I always had a lot of fun, and I think they did, too. Over the years I probably learned more from them than they did from me.

Quite frequently I would ask: "Can I borrow that?" They were always so pleased that the chef of such a well-known place as the Home Port would borrow a recipe or a technique from them.

I always had themes for my demonstrations—I showed them how to make my chowder, cut and broil fish, and boil lobsters. And then we did desserts. They all wanted to know the secret of the key lime pie. Of course, I was obliged to share it with them. It's funny because it is one of the easiest pies to make: You just mix everything together and pour it in the crust, and pop it in the refrigerator. It's that simple. I was mixing everything up when this tiny hand in the back went up. "Mr. Holtham, Mr. Holtham," this wonderful little gray-haired woman called out. "Are you going to make us eat raw eggs?" I paused. I had always used raw eggs in the pie and not given it a second thought. "Aren't you worried about salmonella?" she asked.

After they had gone and dinner was over that night, it was time to start making the pies for the next day. I thought about what that sweet little old lady said and started using pasteurized egg yolks. There is no difference in the taste or texture, and it is one less thing to worry about.

Blueberry Pie

Always a favorite, this pie can be made year-round thanks to the availability of frozen blueberries. I always prepared my pies with a complete top crust, but this pie also looks—and tastes—great with a lattice construction.

2 10-inch traditional piecrusts (page 206)

5 cups wild Maine blueberries

¾ cup sugar

1 teaspoon lemon juice

1 teaspoon lemon zest

1 tablespoon cold butter, cut into 6 pieces

2 tablespoons tapioca (quick-cook tapioca granules)

Pinch of salt

3 tablespoons milk

1. Preheat oven to 350°F.
2. Roll out one piecrust and place in a 10-inch pie dish.
3. Gently mix all the ingredients except milk in a large mixing bowl and pour into the pie dish.
4. Roll out second crust.
5. Wet the rim of the bottom crust with milk.
6. Place the top crust over filling and pinch top and bottom crusts together. Cut air vents in the top crust and brush with milk.
7. Bake for 40 minutes. The crust should be light brown.
8. Remove from oven and sprinkle with sugar. Allow to cool before serving.
9. Serve with ice cream—vanilla is good, but chocolate is even better.

MAKES 1 PIE

A Spoonful of Sugar

The first year I owned the Home Port, I tried to do everything the same way Chet did. That meant getting up at four every morning to do the baking. Well, let's just say I'm not a morning person. I was twenty-eight years old—four in the morning was when I should have been going to bed. Sometimes it felt like I was passing myself on the stairs to my apartment. After about a week of that nonsense, I decided that this was one tradition I was not going to be able to maintain. Instead, I started doing the majority of the baking at night, after dinner. It worked well for me over the years—well, except for one night.

It was one of those crazy nights. We were booked solid, and the people just kept coming. By the time I got to the baking, it was a little later than usual. I always started with the cold pies, the lemon

meringue and the key lime. Those were the easiest. I would knock out about twenty of each and get them into the refrigerator, then go to work on the pies that took a little longer: apple and pecan and blueberry. Next to key lime, the blueberry pie was probably the most popular. We used these wonderful wild blueberries from up in Maine. It was also my least favorite to make because it took the longest. Making one pie is not terribly difficult, but twenty a night, with all of the rolling, can be a little tiresome after a while. First I'd roll out the bottom crusts and add the blueberries, sugar, butter, and lime juice, and then I'd roll out the top crusts and very carefully cover them.

I was in the middle of filling the blueberry pies when the Seward boys, Doug and Dave, showed up at the back door. They were quite the entrepreneurs: They ran a little grocery store across the street and a seasonal garbage route. Every night they came by with their trash truck and collected all of the garbage at the restaurant and along the beach. They had a pretty good thing going. At night, usually around midnight, they would come by to get our trash. Sometimes they would come in and have a piece of fresh pie and we would chat for a while. Usually I would have finished making the pies and would be cleaning up when they showed up—but not that night. That night I was still in the middle of things.

We chatted for a little while and then they were on their way. I rolled out top crusts and put them on the blueberry pies, and in the oven they went. When the timer went off, I took them out and started to sprinkle the sugar on top, because that's what Chet did, and was overcome with the feeling that I had forgotten something—forgotten to put the sugar in the filling, to be exact.

As soon as one of the pies was cool enough to taste, I took a little bite. My fears were confirmed. I had indeed forgotten to put the sugar in the filling—and blueberry pie isn't terribly good without sugar. I thought about what to do for a while. I could either try to somehow fix the pies I had already made, or spend another couple hours doing them over. It was already very late and I was tired, so I convinced myself I could fix them. I started scooping spoonfuls of sugar into the chevrons I always cut in the tops of the crusts to vent the steam, and all but covered the crust with sugar. I tasted it again. It wasn't bad. It wasn't that good, not like they usually are, but it wasn't bad.

The next day I watched anxiously when the first piece of blueberry pie went out. No complaints. Then another and another, and no one said anything. I figured I was in the clear. Wrong.

Brenda had been a waitress at the Home Port since I went to work for Chet back in 1967. She knew the restaurant as well as anyone, probably even better than me at that point. She and her cousin, Linda, helped me out a lot those first few years. In the middle of dinner service that night, Brenda came into the kitchen right after she had gone out with some blueberry pie. I knew I was in trouble.

"Mrs. So and So at table 14 is wondering about the blueberry pie," Brenda said. I knew the customer's name immediately. She and her husband had a house in Chilmark and ate at the Home Port at least once a week. She always had the blueberry pie. "What did she want to know?" I replied wearily. "She was thinking, maybe, you used native blueberries instead of the regular ones in the pie tonight because it is a little more tart than usual." "Bingo," I said. "I did use native blueberries," which was, of course, a lie, but one I thought I could live with. "I guess I should have put a little more sugar in than usual," I told Brenda, who relayed the message, much to the customer's satisfaction. Brenda knew I was full of it, though. Fortunately, that was the only complaint about my sugarless pies. Since then, I've always made sure to put sugar in the pies.

Peanut Butter Pie

1½ cups (8 ounces) whipped cream cheese

1⅓ cups (1 14-ounce can) condensed milk

1 cup peanut butter (chunky or smooth, your choice)

1 teaspoon vanilla extract

½ cup nondairy whipped topping

Chocolate syrup

1 10-inch graham cracker piecrust (page 207)

Chet Cummens was the first person I ever knew to make peanut butter pie. I'm not saying he invented it, but for a long time his was the only one around.

The best thing about peanut butter pie is there is no baking required. Just be sure to let it chill for 24 hours before serving.

1. In a large glass bowl, combine cream cheese, condensed milk, peanut butter, and vanilla extract.
2. When thoroughly mixed, fold in nondairy whipped topping.
3. Generously drizzle chocolate syrup over piecrust.
4. Pour mixture into piecrust and refrigerate overnight.
5. Drizzle chocolate syrup over top of pie before serving.

MAKES 1 PIE

To Err or Not to Err

Way back when I first went to work at the Home Port, Chet Cummens's pecan pie was, without a doubt, one of the most popular desserts going. He sold dozens of pies a week straight from his bakeshop. People went so crazy over his pecan pie, he could hardly get a moment's peace without someone pestering him for his recipe. Okay, that might be a slight exaggeration, though if you asked him, you might think it was true.

Now, for many chefs, it is hard to just hand someone a recipe for something you worked so long and hard to perfect. Plus, if people are making something at home, that means they aren't buying it from you—basically a no-win situation.

Well, one summer it looked as if Chet had come around. Being the genius restaurateur that he was, he had his coveted pecan pie recipe printed on the back of the lunch menus (the Home Port was still serving lunch then). Like the lunches we served, the menus were simple, printed on colored cardstock, intended for people to take home with them. As soon as he put the recipe on the back of the menus, however, a funny thing happened: People would come in and say, "I followed your recipe to the letter, but it just didn't come out the way

yours does." Chet got that a lot, actually. He would smile slyly and shrug his shoulders and speculate as to where they went wrong.

By following the recipe on the menu, people found they were getting a soupy and less sweet-tasting pie. Chet always claimed that it was a printer's error, though, of course, it was never corrected.

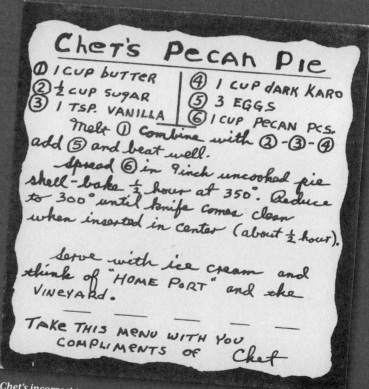

Chet's *incorrect* pecan pie recipe on the back of the Home Port lunch menu

Pecan Pie

1 cup dark Karo syrup

3 eggs

1 cup sugar

½ cup melted butter

¼ teaspoon vanilla extract

2 cups pecans

1 9-inch traditional piecrust (page 206)

Anne Fay, a good friend and neighbor, occasionally would drive over from her home in Vineyard Haven, and she and my wife, Madeline, would go for a brisk walk through the hills surrounding Menemsha. I knew that she loved my pecan pie, so one morning I gave her a whole pie to take home with her. The next morning she called Madeline to thank us for the pie. I could hear her laughing almost hysterically through the phone from across the room. What struck her as so funny was that she managed to eat almost the entire pie as she made the short drive from Menemsha to Vineyard Haven. She said she had pie everywhere—it took her half an hour just to get it off the steering wheel.

1. Preheat oven to 400°F.
2. Combine ingredients in a large mixing bowl. Beat with an electric beater for 1 minute.
3. Place piecrust in a 9-inch pie plate.
4. Pour filling into crust. Bake for 15 minutes.
5. Reduce heat to 350°F and bake for 30 minutes.
6. Allow to cool for 1 hour before serving. Serve with ice cream (vanilla, chocolate, or mocha) and a large dollop of whipped cream.

MAKES 1 PIE

Chocolate Mint Pie

When I worked at Anthony's Pier 4 in Boston in the '70s, this pie was one of their most popular dessert offerings. For some reason I never served it at the Home Port, but it was always one of my favorites.

1. Preheat oven to 325°F.
2. Heat 1 inch of water in a heavy saucepan.
3. Put chocolate chips and butter in a glass bowl and place bowl above (not touching) the water. Stir chocolate chips and butter until melted.
4. Remove bowl from heat and add condensed milk.
5. Whisk eggs and add to mixture. Stir thoroughly.
6. Add milk and peppermint and stir.
7. Pour filling into crust. Bake for 40 minutes or until middle is soft but firm.
8. Cool for 4 hours before serving. Top with whipped cream.

MAKES 1 PIE

¾ cup chocolate chips (milk chocolate or sweet baking)

5 tablespoons butter

1⅓ cups (1 14-ounce can) condensed milk

3 eggs

½ cup milk, warmed

1 teaspoon peppermint flavoring

1 10-inch graham cracker piecrust (page 207)

Nantucket Cranberry Pie

2 cups cranberries
½ cup pecans
1½ cups sugar
¾ cup butter, melted
1 teaspoon almond extract
1 teaspoon orange extract
1 cup flour
2 eggs, beaten

This recipe was given to me by my good friend Pat Lynch. She served it at a dinner party some thirty years ago, and I've been making it ever since. Cherries, blueberries, or rhubarb can be substituted for cranberries.

1. Preheat oven to 350°F.
2. Combine cranberries, pecans, and ½ cup sugar in a large mixing bowl.
3. In a separate bowl, mix melted butter, almond extract, orange extract, remaining sugar, flour, and eggs.
4. Combine mixtures and stir gently.
5. Pour into a glass pie plate. Bake for 45 minutes (longer if berries are frozen).

MAKES 1 PIE

Chocolate Bread Pudding

This recipe is dedicated to my wife, Madeline. Sometimes I wonder if she loves chocolate more than she loves me.

1. Bring heavy cream and sugar to a boil in a heavy-bottomed saucepan. Remove from heat as soon as mixture begins to boil and stir until sugar is dissolved.
2. Add chocolate and stir until chocolate is melted.
3. In a large glass bowl, whisk eggs, egg yolks, vanilla, and milk.
4. Slowly add cream and chocolate mix to glass bowl, stirring constantly until well blended.
5. Add bread cubes to bowl, stirring gently until mixture covers bread. Let stand for 1 hour.
6. Preheat oven to 325°F.
7. After mixture has stood for 1 hour, pour into an 8 x 8-inch (2 quart) buttered baking dish.
8. Place baking dish inside a large roasting pan. Add water to roasting pan until it reaches halfway up the sides of the baking dish.
9. Bake for 1 hour or until filling is set.
10. Cool for 20 minutes. Serve warm with a generous scoop of vanilla ice cream.

SERVES 6–8

Options: Top with white chocolate sauce, caramel sauce, butterscotch sauce, or hard sauce.

2 cups heavy cream

¾ cup sugar

1½ cups semisweet chocolate

3 eggs

3 egg yolks

1 teaspoon vanilla extract

2 cups milk (2% or whole)

6 cups cubed day-old bread (baguette, challah, or brioche), cut into 1- to 2-inch pieces

Time to Make the Sweet Rolls

It was early on a Saturday morning. Really early. I was dead asleep after a good night out when Esther Cummens came into the bunkhouse and shook me awake. "Get up," she said. "You need to make the sweet rolls."

Chet Cummens baking, 1965

Chet's pecan rolls were legendary. On weekend mornings just about all of Menemsha and Chilmark, and half of Vineyard Haven, would come to the back door for his sweet rolls. It didn't hurt any that, thanks to some creative ventilation, the entire village smelled of the delicious confections just as everyone was waking up. Chet's sweet rolls were so good, he had a hard time keeping the staff from eating them all. Chet couldn't make them fast enough, which, I think, is probably why he stopped making them.

Making those sweet rolls that morning was about the only baking I did before I bought the Home Port. Chet loved to bake. That was the one thing he insisted on doing himself. It took an emergency to tear him away. When Esther came in to get me up, she said their son Chuck had been in a minor car accident. He was, fittingly enough, out delivering some sweet rolls and missed a turn and drove the restaurant van into a tree. He wasn't hurt, thankfully, though the van was a little smashed up. I think the tree got the worst of it. Chet said when he got there, Chuck was sitting on the side of the road eating a sweet roll.

During the years I was an employee at the Home Port, I spent plenty of time in Chet's bakeshop— watching. I started doing it my first year there, when I was still the Night Man. Living in the bunkhouse, there wasn't a whole lot to do. I was never really a beach person. I went from time to time with everyone, mainly to look at the girls, but it was not something I enjoyed doing every day like some people. So while everyone was down at the beach, I would go into the kitchen and talk with Chet and help him out when he needed it.

When I decided I might want to make a career out of cooking, I really started paying attention to what Chet was doing. I asked questions. So that morning when Chet had to run off and make sure Chuck was okay, I knew what to do. And more importantly, Chet knew I knew what to do. I had seen him do it a thousand times. He already had the dough mixed and ready. All I had to do was roll out the dough and add the sugar, cinnamon, and pecans and put them in the oven. It was quite a thrill to be in Chet's bakeshop unsupervised. It never happened. I felt like a kid left overnight in a toy store. The rolls came out perfectly. I was quite proud of myself.

It took nearly twenty years for people to get over the fact that Chet stopped making his sweet rolls. As late as the early '90s, people would come in the back door on Saturday and Sunday mornings wanting to buy some sweet rolls. They would be shocked when I told them Chet had stopped making them in the early '70s. "That's impossible," they would say. "I had some just last year." Then they would think about it for a second or two. "Or maybe it was the year before that."

Change was never a good thing at the Home Port. That's why anything hardly ever did.

Chet's Pecan Rolls

Dough:

¼ cup warm water

1 package (2¼ teaspoons or ¼ ounce) active dry yeast

½ cup milk, room temperature

5 tablespoons butter, softened

⅓ cup sugar

2 eggs, room temperature

1 egg yolk, room temperature

1 teaspoon vanilla extract

½ teaspoon salt

3½ cups all-purpose flour

Filling:

3 tablespoons butter, melted

½ cup packed light brown sugar

1 tablespoon ground cinnamon

1 cup chopped pecans

Chet cranked these wonderful morsels out every weekend morning, selling them by the dozen out the back door when they weren't gobbled up by the staff. I recommend making two batches—a single batch will be gone before you know it—and freezing a portion for later.

1. Combine warm water and yeast in an electric mixer bowl. Stir to dissolve yeast and let sit for 5 minutes.

2. Add remaining dough ingredients and mix with whisk attachment on low speed until thoroughly blended.

3. Switch mixer to dough hook and mix on medium speed for 4 minutes. The dough should be smooth and elastic and not stick to the sides of the bowl. If the dough is too wet, add a little more flour.

4. Shape dough into a ball and place in a large buttered bowl. Cover with plastic wrap. Allow dough to proof in a warm place (approximately 80°F) until the ball has doubled in size (approximately 90 minutes).

5. Punch down the dough and place on a lightly floured flat surface large enough to roll out the dough. Allow to sit for 20 minutes.

6. Roll out dough into a 24 x 10-inch rectangle. Brush dough with 2 tablespoons melted butter and sprinkle with sugar, cinnamon, and pecans.

7. Starting at the top, roll dough toward you. When finished rolling, seal the ends by folding them toward the center. Cut into 16 equal pieces.

8. Place rolls into individual greased molds of a cupcake pan. Drizzle rolls with 1 tablespoon melted butter and let rise in a warm place for 1 hour.

9. Preheat oven to 375°F.

10. Bake approximately 30 minutes until golden brown.

MAKES 16 ROLLS

The Back Door

The Home Port's Back Door was one of Menemsha's best-kept secrets for years. I wish I could lay claim to the idea, but Chet Cummens gets all of the credit. All I did was capitalize on his brilliance, expanding it as the secret slowly got out and demand increased, turning it into a huge part of the Home Port's cachet.

It all started in the late '60s, after Chet decided to focus on dinner service. He was already selling baked goods out of the restaurant's back door. People would come in and pick up one of his sweet creations, chat with everyone for a while, and be on their way. From time to time the locals wanted something a little more savory than sweet rolls or pie. At the time, the Home Port was about the only place to get something to eat in Menemsha. Some of the local fishermen and constructions workers—friends of Chet's—would pop in during the day and Chet would make them something, like a lobster salad sandwich, and they would go down by the

water and eat their lunch. It was more of a convenience for a few people than anything else—a convenience Chet was only more than happy to provide.

By 1977, when I took over ownership of the Home Port, the Back Door had blossomed into something more than a convenience for a few people. The secret was starting to get out. When Chet sold me the restaurant, he was serving forty to fifty dinners a night through the Back Door. He offered the entire menu, but at a lower price than in the dining room—a practice I staunchly upheld. I could not, in good conscience, charge customers the full-service price for their meal when I was not providing full service. Today, I see so many places that offer take-out service but at the same price as what people would pay if they went in and sat down and were waited on by someone.

During the first few years I owned the Home Port, the Back Door service continued to grow modestly. Back then, people would literally come in the back door of the restaurant and we'd box up everything for them while they waited right there in the kitchen, on the edge of all the chaos. It wasn't until the late '80s and early '90s, when Martha's Vineyard suddenly became the place to be—Hollywood East, as so many people called it— that our Back Door business fully evolved. Dinner reservations were at a premium. People were making reservations weeks, months, even a year in advance. For someone calling that night, or walking in, it was often all but impossible to get a table unless you were willing to eat really early or really late. We always did our best to accommodate everyone, though. It's not good business to turn people away unless you absolutely have to. If I had my way, everyone would get a table. But there was only so much space inside, even with the couple of small expansion projects I undertook over the years. Really, the only place I could expand was outside—so that's exactly what I did.

After I put in the patio off the back of the restaurant, Back Door business boomed—to the point where I was forced to remodel the kitchen to allow for a dedicated line for Back Door service. But it was always more than just a take-out window. Customers would come and sit outside, with a front-row seat for the spectacular sunsets, and have their dinner. The patio became the place to see and be seen, more so even than the dining room. For every celebrity sitting in the dining room, there were two or three sitting outside, just part of the crowd. Over the years we added a raw bar and more tables, until the Back Door and the patio became as much a part of the Home Port mystique as sitting down to dinner in the dining room. It's not much of a secret anymore.

Metric Conversion Tables

Metric U.S. Approximate Equivalents

Liquid Ingredients

METRIC	U.S. MEASURES	METRIC	U.S. MEASURES
1.23 ML	¼ TSP.	29.57 ML	2 TBSP.
2.36 ML	½ TSP.	44.36 ML	3 TBSP.
3.70 ML	¾ TSP.	59.15 ML	¼ CUP
4.93 ML	1 TSP.	118.30 ML	½ CUP
6.16 ML	1¼ TSP.	236.59 ML	1 CUP
7.39 ML	1½ TSP.	473.18 ML	2 CUPS OR 1 PT.
8.63 ML	1¾ TSP.	709.77 ML	3 CUPS
9.86 ML	2 TSP.	946.36 ML	4 CUPS OR 1 QT.
14.79 ML	1 TBSP.	3.79 L	4 QTS. OR 1 GAL.

Dry Ingredients

METRIC	U.S. MEASURES	METRIC		U.S. MEASURES
2 (1.8) G	$\frac{1}{16}$ OZ.	80 G		$2\frac{4}{5}$ OZ.
3½ (3.5) G	⅛ OZ.	85 (84.9) G		3 OZ.
7 (7.1) G	¼ OZ.	100 G		3½ OZ.
15 (14.2) G	½ OZ.	115 (113.2) G		4 OZ.
21 (21.3) G	¾ OZ.	125 G		4½ OZ.
25 G	⅞ OZ.	150 G		5¼ OZ.
30 (28.3) G	1 OZ.	250 G		$8\frac{7}{8}$ OZ.
50 G	1¾ OZ.	454 G	1 LB.	16 OZ.
60 (56.6) G	2 OZ.	500 G	1 LIVRE	$17\frac{3}{5}$ OZ.

INDEX

Acknowledgments

First, I would like to thank my lovely wife, Madeline, who encouraged me to do something with my time now that I am retired, and allowed me to take over the kitchen table for more than the year it took to put this book together.

To my children, Jessica, Michael, and Megan, who encouraged me to write this book, and whose help was invaluable along the way, thank you.

A big thank-you to my sister, Judy, for deciding to spend the summer of '67 at home, and to my mother who not so subtly suggested I spend that summer away from home. Without them I would not have gone to the Vineyard that fateful summer.

Thank you to everyone in the Cummens family, who became as much my family as my own. You showed me how to do it. All I had to do was do my best not to mess it up too badly.

I would like to thank the Athanas family, under whose tutelage I learned what it took to become a successful restaurateur and businessman.

A great big thank-you to the thousands of employees without whose hard work, dedication, and good humor the success of the Home Port would not have been possible.

To the local fish markets, Poole's, Larson's, and the Net Result, thank you for making sure I always had the pick of the catch.

For the more than two million customers I had the privilege of serving over the thirty-two years of my stewardship of the Home Port, many of whom became friends over the years, thank you for coming back year after year and bringing your friends and family.

Thank you to Mary Norris and all the good people at the Globe Pequot Press who made this book a reality; my agent, Lorin Rees, who believed in this book and saw it to fruition; A. D. Minnick, who came up with the words when I couldn't; Susan Tobey White, for her wonderful illustrations; and Mike Buytas for his photographic talents.

After thirty-two years as owner and chef of the Home Port, it is my pleasure to pass its legacy to the capable hands of Bob and Sarah Nixon, where it will endure, I am sure, for many, many more years to come. I wish them both all the success in the world.

—*Will Holtham*

About the Author

Will Holtham has been a chef and restaurateur for more than forty years. He began his career at the Home Port in 1967, mopping the restaurant floors. Over the next five years he climbed the ranks of the restaurant's kitchen staff, and in 1977 was offered the opportunity of a lifetime: ownership of the Home Port. He served as chef until his retirement in 2008. He also owned the Square Rigger restaurant and legendary The Bite, both on Martha's Vineyard. He divides his time between the Cape, Maine, and South Carolina, where he continues to cook for friends and family.

About the Illustrator

Susan Tobey White spent the summer at Martha's Vineyard in 1972 and has been returning ever since to visit friends and enjoy the island. Every visit includes a meal at the Home Port. She is the owner of High Street Studio and Gallery in Belfast, Maine, where she teaches and shows her own work and that of others.